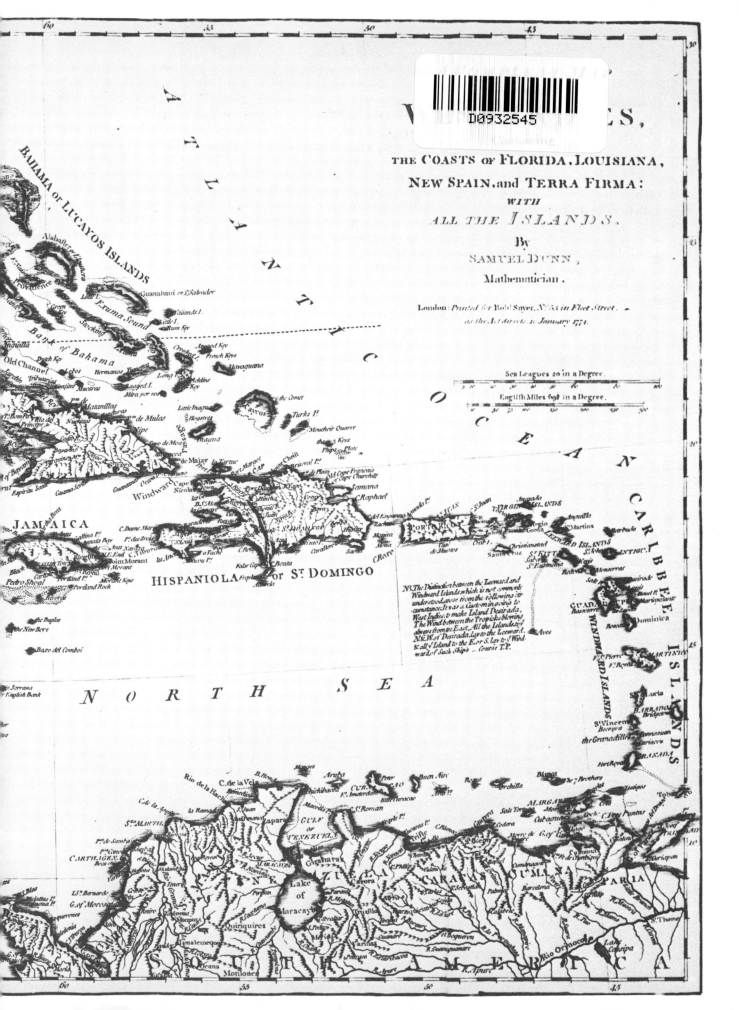

THE JOURNAL OF GIDEON OLMSTED

THE JOURNAL OF
Gideon Olmsted

Adventures of a Sea Captain during the American Revolution

A FACSIMILE

Introduction and reading text by GERARD W. GAWALT
American Revolution Bicentennial Office

Coda by CHARLES W. KREIDLER
Georgetown University

LIBRARY OF CONGRESS   WASHINGTON   1978

Slipcase: *Môle Saint Nicolas, Haiti. Line engraving by Nicolas and Jeanne-Françoise Ozanne, about 1780.*
Endpapers: *"A Compleat Map of the West Indies" by Samuel Dunn, London, 1774. From* The American Military Pocket Atlas, *1776.*
Frontispiece: *Portrait of Captain Gideon Olmsted, painted about 1810.*

LIBRARY OF CONGRESS CATALOGING IN PUBLICATION DATA

Olmsted, Gideon, 1749–1845.
    The journal of Gideon Olmsted; adventures of a sea captain during the American Revolution.

    The facsim. of the author's journal was made from a
ms. located in the Frederick Law Olmsted papers in the
Manuscript Division of the Library of Congress.
    Includes bibliographical references.
    1. Olmsted, Gideon, 1749–1845. 2. United States—
History—Revolution, 1775–1783—Personal narratives.
3. United States—History—Revolution, 1775–1783—Naval
operations. 4. Privateering. 5. Shipmasters—United
States—Biography. I. United States. Library of
Congress. Manuscript Division. II. Title.
E207.05A32   973.3'5 [B]   77-608234
ISBN 0-8444-0251-6

ADVISORY COMMITTEE

Library of Congress
American Revolution Bicentennial Program

FOREWORD

GIDEON OLMSTED has long occupied a place of distinction in the annals of American jurisprudence. His 30-year litigation over the prize money from the sale of the British sloop *Active* set an early precedent for the supremacy of federal over state authority. The events leading up to his monumental court battle, however, have remained relatively obscure. This volume chronicles the six-month period of imprisonment and mutiny which precipitated Olmsted's extended legal proceedings.

The journal, produced here both in facsimile and in an edited version, offers not only a provocative account of the adventures of a swashbuckling privateersman but also insight into the history of the English language in America. Written before Webster's standardization of American orthography, it is a prime source of information about certain aspects of colonial pronunciation. The Library is especially grateful to Dr. Charles W. Kreidler of Georgetown University for his enlightening essay on the linguistic significance of the journal and for compiling the glossary. Professor Kreidler, who heads Georgetown's program in applied linguistics, is a distinguished scholar who has published widely in his field.

Olmsted's journal, published here for the first time, has been prepared by Dr. Gerard W. Gawalt, specialist in legal history for the American Revolution Bicentennial Office, as a part of the Library of Congress Bicentennial program. This program has, from its inception, been committed to rescuing important primary and rare secondary sources of the revolutionary era from undeserved obscurity. In 1972 the Library published *English Defenders of American Freedoms, 1774–1778*, an annotated collection of scarce pamphlets written by British advocates of the American position; in 1975 it published *A Decent Respect to the Opinions of Mankind*, a selection of addresses, letters, and petitions justifying American actions and issued by the Continental Congress between 1774 and 1776. The first two volumes of the Library's largest documentary publication project, *Letters of Delegates to Congress, 1774–1789*, will be off the press in 1977. It is hoped that these offerings, together with other published facsimiles, bibliographies, and guides to revolutionary era manuscripts, graphics, maps, and charts in the Library's collections, as well as the papers given at the Library's five Bicentennial symposia, 1972–1976, will increase our familiarity with the world of our forebears from the American Revolution and sharpen our understanding of our cultural heritage.

Elizabeth Hamer Kegan
Assistant Librarian of Congress
for American and Library Studies

CONTENTS

The British sloop Active. *Engraving by Carington Bowles,
London, 1783. Reproduced through the courtesy of the
National Maritime Museum, London, England.*

INTRODUCTION

No one suspected on December 15, 1778, when the standing Committee on Appeals of the Continental Congress ruled in his favor, that Gideon Olmsted and the captured British sloop *Active* would become the focus of one of the earliest and most significant efforts in American history to resolve the issue of states' rights. More than 30 years later Olmsted won a landmark case against Pennsylvania in the federal courts, but not before the bounds of national power had been severely tested. The legal history of the *Active* case and its importance for appellate law are well known.[1] Olmsted's activities leading up to his court career, however, have been obscure.

Olmsted's journal, published here for the first time,[2] reveals previously unknown and dramatic details of a promising trading voyage turned into a nightmare of captivity, torture, privation, mutiny, and protracted legal entanglement. Located in the Frederick Law Olmsted Papers in the Manuscript Division, the journal—along with a typescript noting only that it was given to Frederick Law Olmsted by his great uncle Gideon—has gone unnoticed by scholars. But with the journal's discovery, Olmsted's incredible tenacity in pursuing his legal and financial rights is more understandable.

Gideon Olmsted grew up in East Hartford, Conn., where he was born on February 12, 1749. When he was 20 he shipped out as a seaman apprentice and for the next five years sailed the Atlantic seaboard and through the West Indies. Returning to East Hartford just as war broke out in neighboring Massachusetts, he served nearly a year at Boston in the militia regiment of Col. Joseph Spencer. In April 1776 young Olmsted mustered out of the army, eager for the spoils of privateering. A year at sea provided him with sufficient funds to purchase a one-third share in a ship, the *Seaflower*, at Westerly, R.I. Gideon, his brother Aaron, and Abraham Miller paid £189 for the vessel of 75 tons burden and brought her back to Hartford to be loaded for a trip to the West Indies.[3]

Captain Olmsted must have envisioned a lucrative voyage as he sailed from Hartford on December 19, 1777, with a cargo of horses, tobacco, onions, barrel hoops, and bricks, bound for Port Louis on the island of Guade-loupe. At first the journey was as normal as wartime conditions would permit. But on April 7, 1778, as the *Seaflower* was returning to Connecticut with molasses, coffee, tea, and salt,[4] the British warship *Weir* captured vessel and crew without firing a shot—triggering for Olmsted a six-month ordeal that saw him twice a prisoner aboard ship, in jail at Haiti, and finally as instigator of a successful mutiny on the British sloop *Active*. Heading for Egg Harbor, N.J., in September 1778 to libel his prize, Olmsted was stopped by the Pennsylvania brig *Convention*, whose captain claimed the *Active* for Pennsylvania, since it still carried British papers. Olmsted protested, but in vain.

The *Active* reached Philadelphia on September 15, 1778, and was libeled on September 18. The case was tried by jury before Judge George Ross of the court of admiralty for the port of Philadelphia. On November 5, 1778, one-quarter ($24,700) of the prize money resulting from the sale of the ship and cargo was awarded to Gideon Olmsted and the three other ex-prisoners who had captured the *Active* on September 6; the rest was to be divided between the state and the owners of the *Gerard*—in sight when the *Convention* took the *Active*—and the officers and crews of the *Convention* and the privateer.

Without friends and in foreign territory, Olmsted turned to a fellow Connecticut resident, Benedict Arnold, who was then military commander of Philadelphia.[5] Arnold, along with Stephen Collins, a Philadelphia merchant, provided Olmsted with the financial backing and political influence needed to appeal the case (*Thomas Houston, Esq. etc. appellees* adv. *Gideon Olmsted, etc. appellants*) to the Committee on Appeals of the Continental Congress. On December 15, 1778, the committee ordered that the entire proceeds of the sale be paid to Olmsted and the three crew members who had assisted him. Two weeks later Judge Ross refused to obey the congressional order to release the money. Olmsted's journal ends here, but his legal maneuvers were just beginning.

The issue between the Continental Congress and the state of Pennsylvania was clearly drawn. The Committee on Appeals, acting under a congressional resolve of 1775, had made a ruling on appeal, which the state of Pennsylvania would not obey. To submit, the state contended, would be a violation of state law, which prohibited appeal from a jury trial on questions of fact. But Congress did not want to endanger the war effort by alienating Pennsylvania, or, for that matter, Massachusetts and New Hampshire, which held similar views regarding appeal.[6] Short of force there was nothing the committee could do when its January 4, 1779, injunction against payment of the proceeds to the admiralty court was ignored and the state's share was turned over to David Rittenhouse, treasurer of the state of Pennsylvania. Benedict Arnold, in a postscript to a letter to the congressional appeals committee on the very eve of that action, anticipated the course the case was to take:

> I am informed from good authority that a member of the Assembly has applied to get the money paid into his hands, and if he should succeed in this it will probably be paid into the Treasury, and the claimants will have the whole State to contend with in their own government.[7]

But Arnold's warning went unheeded. Congress apparently was not willing at that time to meet the issue head on and, after a few mild protests, dropped the matter. Gideon Olmsted would not.

Bringing his family to Philadelphia, Olmsted continued his efforts to collect the full compensation awarded him by the congressional appeals committee. He returned to his career as a ship captain to support his household and began a series of petitions to the Pennsylvania Assembly which did not end until he was 59 years old. By that time all the other parties originally involved in the case had died or lost interest.

Olmsted nearly succeeded in 1803, when Richard Peters, judge of the United States district court of Pennsylvania, ruled in his favor. But once again the state interposed itself between a national court ruling and a state resident. On April 2, 1803, the Pennsylvania Assembly passed an act expressly forbidding the execution of Judge Peters' decree. Legally, their act was based on rulings by Judge Ross in 1778 and by Thomas McKean, chief justice of the state supreme court. McKean ruled that the decree of the Committee on Appeals had been "extra-judicial, erroneous, and Void" because of the absence of a jury to determine the facts, despite the clear wording of the congressional resolve of November 25, 1775, providing "That in all cases, an appeal shall be allowed to the congress" for cases concerning prize captures.

Partisan politics and fears of impeachment prevented further federal action against the government of Pennsylvania. Republican newspapers, such as the *Aurora*, hailed the assembly's decision and warned that "if the Federal Courts, under the insidious cover of legal forms and technical decisions, can legislate for the separate States, or set aside their legislative acts, or bring State independency under the control of jurisdiction, the spirit of the Union is destroyed and the liberties of the people will be brought to the footstool of aristocracy."[8] With this decision coming shortly after the ruling handed down in *Marbury* v. *Madison* and when possible impeachment of federal judges Richard Peters and Samuel Chase was being freely discussed, Peters declined to proceed against Pennsylvania in what would only be interpreted as a move by the "Federalist judiciary" against a "Republican legislature."[9]

Gideon Olmsted, himself, was well aware of the political implications surrounding the case. In his file along with the journal in the Frederick Law Olmsted papers is a brief account—prepared for the meeting of the Pennsylvania Assembly at Lancaster early in 1808—of circumstances leading up to the mutiny and his subsequent legal actions. In it he contends that his early court losses stemmed from his inability to retain Whig lawyers and, further, that the reason Congress did not jail Judge Ross for contempt of Congress was because the Continental Army was completely dependent on Pennsylvania for provisions.

Finally, in 1809 the Assembly of Pennsylvania gave in and agreed to pay Olmsted. But not before the federal marshal, enforcing a writ of attachment in pursuance of a peremptory *mandamus* handed down by U.S. Supreme Court Chief Justice John Marshall, arrested the heirs of David Rittenhouse[10] despite the active opposition of massed Pennsylvania militia called out by the governor of Pennsylvania to protect them. Later, Supreme Court Justice Bushrod Washington, nephew of George Washington, sentenced the involved militia officers to fines and prison terms for resisting federal authority. Precedence for predominance of federal over state law had been established. And Gideon Olmsted's persistence had been justified. Chief Justice Marshall, in delivering the opinion of the court, put it this way:

> If the legislatures of the several states may, at will, annul the judgments
> of the courts of the United States, and destroy the rights acquired
> under those judgments, the constitution itself becomes a solemn mockery;
> and the nation is deprived of the means of enforcing its laws by the
> instrumentality of its own tribunals. So fatal a result must be deprecated
> by all; and the people of Pennsylvania, not less than the citizens of every
> other state, must feel a deep interest in resisting principles so destructive of
> the union, and in averting consequences so fatal to themselves.[11]

Olmsted was not handsomely rewarded for his resistance. Monetarily he probably would have been better off had he accepted the one-fourth offer made in 1778. He received in total $35,718.47, but his expenses over the years for the court battles had amounted to $22,873.44.[12] In 1810 Olmsted left Philadelphia for Connecticut, where he died in 1845.

Presented here is a facsimile of Olmsted's journal, apparently written from memory shortly after he lost the first round of court cases to Judge Ross. Each page is juxtaposed with the corresponding page of an edited version, in which spelling and capitalization have been modernized and geographic names corrected where the intent was clear. Punctuation has been inserted only insofar as necessary to clarify the author's meaning. Word usage and syntax have been left unaltered.

In brief, the sequence of events is this: *Seaflower*, returning to Connecticut from Guadeloupe, is captured by *Weir*. Olmsted and his men are taken prisoner. Released off St. Ann's Bay, Jamaica, they land at an estate and in about two weeks get a boat for Môle St. Nicolas, Haiti. The boat is captured off Haiti by the *Niger*'s tender; they are taken into Kingston, Jamaica, and set at liberty. Olmsted makes his way to Port-au-Prince, Haiti, where he signs on *Polly*, a French privateer. At sea they battle *Ostrich* and *Lowestoffe's Prize*. *Polly* is captured, Olmsted and crew again taken prisoner. Jailed at Montego Bay but "set at liberty" within a few days, Olmsted joins British ship *Active* "as a hand to do my duty to work the sloop to New York."[13] He plans and carries out a mutiny. *Active*, with Olmsted in command, is intercepted and claimed as a prize by *Convention*, an armed ship owned by Pennsylvania.

What follows is Olmsted's own graphic account of this remarkable Revolutionary War sea adventure.

NOTES

[1] In an address before the Yale Law School, June 26, 1888, U.S. Supreme Court Justice Stanley Matthews is quoted as having said "This [the *Active* case] appears to have been the first case in which the supremacy of the Constitution was enforced by judicial tribunals against the assertion of State authority." J. C. Bancroft Davis, *United States Reports. Cases Adjudged in the U. S. Supreme Court at October Term, 1888*, vol. 131 (New York: Banks & Brothers, 1889), app., p. xxxiv n. See also Charles Warren, *The Supreme Court in United States History*, vol. 1 (Boston: Little, Brown, and Company, 1922), pp. 366–99.

For legal aspects of the case see *United States* v. *Judge Peters* in William Cranch, *Reports of Cases Argued and Adjudged in the Supreme Court of the United States, in February Term, 1809*, 3d ed., vol. 5 (New York: Isaac Riley, 1882), pp. 115–41; *Ross et al. Executors* v. *Rittenhouse* in Alexander J. Dallas, *Reports of Cases Ruled and Adjudged in the Several Courts of the United States and of Pennsylvania*, 2d ed., vol. 2 (New York: Lawyers Co-operative Publishing Company, 1882), pp. 160–68; *Penhallow, et al.* v. *Doane Administrators*, Dallas, *Reports*, vol. 3, pp. 53–120; Charles Page Smith, *James Wilson, Founding Father, 1742–1798* (Chapel Hill: University of North Carolina Press for the Institute of Early American History and Culture, Williamsburg, Va., 1956), pp. 124–28; Gideon Olmsted to Gentlemen of the Committee, January 28, 1808, in Olmsted Papers, Library of Congress; *Proceedings of a General Court Martial for the Trial of Major General Arnold* (New York: J. Munsell, Printer, 1865), pp. 119–28, first published in 1780; see also relevant entries in the *Journals of the Continental Congress:* November 28, 1778; January 19, 21, February 2, 13, 25, March 3, 6, 9, 16, 30, April 6, 9, 19, 24, 28, September 6, 29, October 12, 21, 1779; and January 17 and March 21, 1780; Edmund C. Burnett, ed., *Letters of Members of the Continental Congress*, vol. 4 (Washington: Carnegie Institute and Lord Baltimore Press, 1928, passim; *Sundry Documents Relative to the Claim of Gideon Olmsted Against the Commonwealth of Pennsylvania* (Philadelphia: Printed by Edward Olmsted, 1811).

[2] Olmsted's major biographer, Louis F. Middlebrook, in his *Captain Gideon Olmsted, Connecticut Privateersman, Revolutionary War* (Salem, Mass.: Newcomb & Gauss Co., 1933) makes no mention of this journal and apparently knew nothing of its existence.

[3] See Middlebrook, *Olmsted*, pp. 1–19; also Joseph O. Goodwin, *East Hartford: Its History and Traditions* (Hartford: Case, Lockwood & Brainard Co., 1879), pp. 83–84.

[4] Olmsted journal, p. 27.

[5] Benedict Arnold apparently supported Olmsted's appeal to Congress in return for one-half interest in the ship and cargo, which sold for £47,981 in December 1778. He was ac-

cused of corruption by Pennsylvania in a formal complaint to Congress on January 26, 1779, and after a long series of hearings and a court-martial he was acquitted of all but two minor complaints. George Washington punished him with a reprimand. One of the charges was that of purchasing a lawsuit to profit by its prosecution in connection with Olmsted's claim regarding the *Active*. See Carl Van Doren, *Secret History of the American Revolution* (New York: Viking Press, 1941), pp. 176–77, 188–93; Burnett, *Letters*, vol. 4, p. 44 and passim; *Proceedings of a General Court Martial*, pp. 119–28.

[6] New Hampshire and Massachusetts had similar cases pending in their courts, and like Pennsylvania the state courts were refusing to allow appeals to the Congressional Committee on Appeals. See *Penhallow, et al.* v. *Doane's Administrators*, Dallas, *Reports*, vol. 3, pp. 54–120; John Lowell to John Adams, August 4, 1777, in Charles Lowell, ed., "Letters of John Lowell and Others," *Historical Magazine* 1 (September 1857): 258–59; Richard Francis Upton, *Revolutionary New Hampshire: An Account of the Social and Political Forces Underlying the Transition from Royal Province to American Commonwealth* (1936; reprint ed., New York: Octagon Books, 1971), pp. 114–16.

[7] Davis, *Reports*, vol. 131, app., p. xxx.

[8] *Aurora, for the Country* (Philadelphia), April 11, 1803.

[9] Warren, *Supreme Court*, vol. 1, p. 375.

[10] The heirs were Elizabeth Sergeant and Esther Waters, daughters of David Rittenhouse, the Pennsylvania state treasurer in 1779. Judge Ross had paid Rittenhouse £11,496 in U.S. loan office certificates as the share of the state brig *Convention* from the proceeds of the sloop *Active*. Rittenhouse kept the certificates pending his release by the state for giving a bond of indemnity to protect Ross should he have been compelled to pay that amount to Olmsted. The certificates were then retained by Rittenhouse, descending to his daughters, Mrs. Sergeant and Mrs. Waters. Hence Olmsted's efforts to obtain payment from them. Middlebrook, *Olmsted*, pp. 142–45; *Ross et al. Executors* v. *Rittenhouse*, Dallas, *Reports*, vol. 2, pp. 160–68; *United States* v. *Judge Peters*, Cranch, *Reports*, vol. 5, pp. 118–25.

[11] Cranch, *Reports*, vol. 5, p. 136.

[12] Middlebrook, *Olmsted*, p. 150.

[13] See Middlebrook, *Olmsted*, p. 19, for his account of how Olmsted became a member of the *Active*'s crew.

THE JOURNAL OF GIDEON OLMSTED

A Journal of an Intended Voyage
From New London to Guadeloupe
in the Sloop *Seaflower*

Gideon Olmsted, Commander, Israel Deming, mate.
Seamen were John Buckland, John Hodge, Eliphalet
Forbes, Israel Fox, & Hezekiah Burnham and this journal
kept by Gideon Olmsted.[1]

Thurs., 19th of December 1777, at 4 P.M. put out to sea
with the wind at NW. The 24th had a heavy gale of wind
at N. which lasted for 12 hours. A few days after, spoke
with an American privateer, William Corel, Comnr. January 15th, 1778, got safe into Port Louis at Guadeloupe
and sold my cargo to Mr. Antony Gernat.[2]

A Jurnorl off An Intended voige
From Nulondon to Gaudeloope
In the Sloope Mayflower —
Gideon Olmsted Commaunder
Isrel Demmin Mate Seaymen were
John Buckland John Hodg
Eliflet Jacobs Isrel Fox &
Hezekiah Bronham and cept
By Gideon Olmsted
this 19th of December 1777
At 4 P,M. part out to sey with
the Wind at W:S: the 4 had a
harry gale of wind at W which
larsted for 12 hours a fue Day,
After Spoke with an amarakan
Privitteer William Corel Commor
Jenuary 15th 1778 got Safe into
Portlua at Gaudeloope
And Solde my Cargo to Mr
Antone, Gonordls

Gaudeloupe Granteen melo)
March 20th 1776 at 6 OClk maid
Sale for home April 7th at
Daylite saw two Ships to the Win
of us wee maid all Sail wee cold
At 12 thay were so ny us that
wee Saw Brittish cullors wee stove
two hogsheds of Molases in the
fore hole in order to bring her
by the Starn and pumped it out
at 6 OClk thay come up with us
one wors the Ship Wor of 20 guns
Samuel Williams Commander
from Phaledelfa Bound to the
Bay of Hundoras he tuck us
all a bord of him exsept John
Hody and cep the prife under
his Convoy the Capt yoused me
very well while I wors a bord and
told me that he Shold goe into
Jemeca and wold let us all at

Guadeloupe, Grande Terre Mole, March 20th, 1778, at 6 P.M. made sail for home. April 7th at daylight saw two ships to the SW of us. We made all sail we could. At 12 they were so nigh us that we saw British colors. We stove two hogheads of molasses in the forehold in order to bring her by the stern and pumped it out. At 4 P.M. they came up with us. One was the ship *Weir* of 20 guns, Samuel Williams, Commander, from Philadelphia, bound to the Bay of Honduras. He took us all aboard of him except John Hodge and kept the prize under his convoy.[3] The Capt. used me very well while I was aboard and told me that he should go into Jamaica and would set us all at our liberty and give us all our private venture, and if we came across any French vessel he would put us aboard if we chose. Off Cape Francois we spoke with a French snow.[4] I desired that the Capt. would let us go aboard and go to Cape Francois with the Frenchman. The captain refused and said that he wanted us to condemn the sloop [*Seaflower*].[5] I told him that if he would let the people go I would be contented to go down to Jamaica with him as I thought I was sufficient to condemn her. He told me he had no orders to put prisoners aboard of Frenchmen. The 21th made the north side of Jamaica. The Capt. told me that he should not go into port at Jamaica, but if he could see any boat off the harbors he would [allow ?]

Our libberty and give us all
our project venter and if wee come
a crost any french vessel he wold
sett us a bord if wee choes of cape
bonsway wee spoke with a french
snow & desired that the Capt wold
let us goe a bord and goe to cape from
with the frenchman the Capt refused
And said that he wonted us to condem
the Sloope & told him that if he
wold let the people goe I wold be
contented to goe down to yemeco with
him as I thole & wors so fishon't
to condemn her he told me he had
knew orders to put prisnors a bord
of frenchmen the 21th made the worth
hide of yemeco the Capt told me
that he shold not goe into port at
yemeco but if the cold ley any tite
of the harbors he wold

Me and 4 of my people goe a shore
But must heep my mate and one hand
with him as he wors a going to heeep
the sloope with him he must have them
to Condeam the sloope of tant Ans
wee low a bote a going a long shore
to the windland he put me and 4 people
a bord which wors Eliphlet Forb's
Ixel Sose John Buchland Hezehiah
Burnham they [struck through] the Capt
wold not alow one of the people to
take thear chefts he aloud me to
take my Cheft after taking every
thing out but my cloes the bote
landed us at an astate Colled the
Roge about 6 myles from St Ans
one Gorden a Scothman had the care
of it it wors hinderin by that tyme
wee got a shore the bote wors a going
back to St Ans in the morning after
And told us that wee myte goe with
them I went to Mr Gorden

me and 4 of my people go ashore but must keep my mate and one hand with him as he was agoing to keep the sloop with him. He must have them to condemn the sloop. Off Saint Ann's we saw a boat agoing along shore to the windward. He put me and 4 people aboard which was Eliphalet Forbes, Israel Fox, John Buckland, Hezekiah Burnham. The Capt. would not allow one of the people to take their chests. He allowed me to take my chest after taking everything out but my clothes. The boat landed us at an estate called the Boge about 6 miles from St. Ann's. One Gorden, a Scotchman, had the care of it. It was sundown by that time we got ashore. The boat was agoing back to St. Ann's in the morning after and told us that we might go with them. I went to Mr. Gorden and told him that I should be obliged to him if he would let me and 4 more stay upon his estate that night as we were agoing to St. Ann's the next morning in a boat. He asked me what countrymen we were. I told him that we were Americans. He asked if we came out of that British ship he see off. I told him we did. He asked what he put us ashore for. I told him that we were taken in that sloop that he see with the ship and the Capt. that took us had let us ashore that we might get home as quick as we could for he was bound to the Bay of Honduras. He asked me how we expected to get home. I told him that I expected to find some vessel at St. Ann's that was bound to New York or to some French island. He said he should not harbor any

And told him that I shold be
a bliged to him if he wold let me
And n more stay upon his a state
that wyle as wee ware a going to
St ans the next morneng in a bote
he asked me whot cuntremen wee
ware i told him that wee ware a
mericans he asked if wee came out of
thet Brittish shipe he say es I told
him wee did he asked whot he put us
A shore for I told him that wee
ware taken in thet sloope that he
day with the shipe and the Capt that
tuck us had let us a shore that wee
myte git home as queech as wee could
for he wors bound to the Bay of hondas
he asked me how wee exspected to git home
I told him that I exspected to fynd
sum vessel at St ans that wors bound
to neuyork or to sum french Island
he said he shold not harber any

Rebbels I told him wee cold all
goe to it and that wite ecsept one
who wors lame and wold be glad if he
wold be so kind as to let him stay
And take care of sum thyngs that I
Had in the bote he said if he wors
Able to worke I must take him a long
with us I told him that he wors cept
well he said If he cold not goe he
must stay soe the rest of us set of
wee left Hezekyah Burnham in
the bote who had a boyl on his fut
soe that he cold not put on a shue
wor but jest touch his fut to the
ground at nine a clock that night
we got to it ans but a vary bad
rode we went to a tavern a bout
on hour after Burnham came hobblen
A long which sorpryzd me which I
thote it imposseble for a man so lame
to walk in shuch a bad rode I
asked him whot wors the matter

rebels. I told him we could all go to St. Ann's that night except one who was lame and would be glad if he would be so kind as to let him stay and take care of some things that I had in the boat. He said if he was able to walk I must take him along with us. I told him that he was not well. He said if he could not go he must stay. So the rest of us set off. We left Hezekiah Burnham in the boat who had a boil in his foot so that he could not put on a shoe nor but just touch his foot to the ground. At nine o'clock that night we got to St. Ann's but a very bad road. We went to a tavern. About an hour after, Burnham came hobbling along which surprised me which I thought it impossible for a man so lame to walk in such a bad road. I asked him what was the matter.

He told me that the man that belonged to the estate came down with 2 pistols and told him that he could travel well enough and should go off or he would shoot him. He told him that he could not go, he thought, and pled with the man to let him stay. He said that he would not harbor no rebels and ordered him off. The poor fellow hobbled through mud and water and over stones and stumps. We got a bowl of grog and got into a room by ourselves and drank General Washington's health and hoped that it would be our turn next and lay down upon the floor and went to sleep. The next morning the boat came from St. Ann's with my chest which gave me great pleasure for it had a great many good clothes in it. The next thing was to get away.

he told me that the man that belong
to the a slate came down with a pitsforh
And told him that he cold travel
well a nuf and shold goe of or he
wold shut him he told him that
he cold not goe he thote and pled with
the man to let him stay he said that
he wold not harber know rebbels and
ordred him of the poore fellow hobbled
throu mud and worter and over stones and
stumps wee got a bole of grog and
got into a rume by oure selves and
Dranck Ginnorl Woshingtons
helth and hopeed that it wold
be our turn next and lay down
Upon the floor and went to sleecp
the nexet morning the bote came
from St ans with my chest which
gave me grate gulasure for it had
a grate many good thdes in it
the nexet thyng wors to git a way

Thare wors one Mr John Ordy had a
Vefsel thare and wors a going to Cape Nick
Ulemold and told us that wee myste live
att his hous while he wors rayde to goe
And then wee myste goe with him a bout
14 days after wee set out with him 10
Days out wee got olmost to the Cape
the wigors tender Came a Crofs us a
thinking to make a prise of us as wee
ware moued with a marchant the Cord
Brocke into Kingstoun after wee got
the thay let us at our libberty wee
went a shore but had know mony
nor Credet as wee that but luckely
I found one Mr Robert Crofse who
wors an amarchan who wors very kind
to prisoners and told me that I and
My People myste live at his hous untel
Wee Cold get a Chance to goe to the
Mold wee lived at his hous a bout 10 days

There was one Mr. John Oray had a vessel there and was agoing to Cape St. Nicholas Mole and told us that we might live at his house while he was ready to go and then we might go with him. About 14 days after, we set out with him. 10 days out we got almost to the Cape. The *Niger*'s tender[6] came across us athinking to make a prize of us as we were manned with Americans. She carried us back into Kingston. After we got in they set us at our liberty. We went ashore but had no money nor credit, as we thought. But luckily I found one Mr. Robert Crose who was an American who was very kind to prisoners and told me that I and my people might live at his house until we could get a chance to go to the Mole. We lived at his house about 10 days.

I went aboard a little sloop bound to the Cape, Aaron Marted, Captain. Eliphalet Forbes, Fox & Burnham were with me and was to work for their passage. Buckland went aboard of a French schooner[7] to go to the same place. We sailed the 6th of June. The next day after we sailed, Burnham was taken sick. After we had been out 8 days we put into Port Morant to stop a leak. I carried Hezekiah Burnham ashore to a Dutchman's house and agreed with him to take care of him. I carried him ashore about 4 o'clock and left Fox & Forbes with him. I could not get a doctor to him that night. They both watched with him that night. At 12 o'clock at night he died, it being the 15th of June. I gave £3 for a coffin. An American gentleman

I went a bord a little Sloope bound
to the Cape Aaron Marls Copten
Eliflet Smirbs Sose & Burnham
ware with me and wos to work for thair
pafsedg Buckland went a bord of
a french scon er to gee to the Saine place
we saild the 6 th of Jeune the next Day
after we saild Burnham wos teahon
sick after we had bin out 3 Days we
put into Port Morant to stop a leake
I caryed Hezekiah Burnham a shore
also a Dutchmans horus and agreed with
him to take Care of Him I carey him
a shore about 4 aclock and left
Sose & Smirbs with him I cold not
Git a Doctor to him that night
thay both wotched with him that
night at 12 aclock at night he
Dyde it Being the 15 th of Jeune
I gave £3 for a Corffen
an Amorecan Gentleman

4   5

gave a hute to Dres the Corpes
And Decently Buried him the woman where
he Dyde was a very kised woman and
did not ask any thing for her tobte
I made her a preasent of a pear of
hilk gloves that belonged to to the
Man that hde the west day before
Bucklans Came to us who had bin
brote back by an English Crucer
The 18th wee all went a bord a
French Sloope bound to Port a
Prince Capt Bearey who gave
us owr passed 29 wee got into Lee
yan wee heard of a french Brig at
Portleprince ˄ who were a going to america top wee went to Pt prince
And found a Privettear Braig of 16
Guns which wors owned by Mr
Brofhon and manned with french
Mr Brofhon wors Capt of the priverteer
But she had an American Commis
sion and an american Capt

gave a suit to dress the corpse and decently buried him. The woman where he died was a very kind woman and did not ask anything for her trouble. I made her a present of a pair of silk gloves that belonged . . . to the man that died. The next day John Buckland came to us who had been brought back by an English cruiser. The 18th we all went aboard a French sloop bound to Port-au-Prince, Capt. Bearry, who gave us our passage. 29th we got into Léogâne. We heard of a French brig at Port-au-Prince who was agoing to America. We went to Port-au-Prince and found a privateer brig [*Polly*][8] of 16 guns which was owned by Mr. Proshon and manned with French. Mr. Proshon was Capt. of the privateer but she had an American commission and an American Capt.

He told me if I would go with him he would give me 8 shares and was agoing to cruise to the northward. The first port would be America if he did not take anything off Jamaica. John Buckland shipped as prize master and to draw 3 shares. Israel Fox went aboard with us. Eliphalet Forbes did not go. July 3th hove up and went out. Wednesday July 8th at 2 P.M. off the E end of Jamaica fell in with the *Ostrich*,[9] man of war of 16 guns. Before we came up with one another we were under French colors. She fired a shot athwart us. We hauled down our French colors. We came alongside one another. The ship hailed us and told us to bring to or he would fire into us. We hoisted our Continental colors at our main top gallant head and fired a broadside into her,

He told me if I wold goe with
him he wold give me 8 shares and
wos a going to Cruse to the wword
the furst port wold be Amardha
If he didnot take any thing of
Jeneco John Buchland shiped as
pryse mooster and to drow 3 shares
Five Non went a bord with us
Eliflet Furbs didnot goe
July 3 th hove up and went out
Wedensday yuly 4 th at 2 ℗ M
of the E end of Jeneco fell in with
the Crstreg man of war of 16 guns
before wee came up with one another wee
war under french cullors she fired a shot
a thote us wee holled down our french cullors
wee came a long side one another the ship
holled us and told us to bring two or he wold
fyre into us wee histed our Conthenortal
Cullors at our main top gallent hed and
fired a brod side unto her

11   6

Which she amedoitsly returned wee ex=
schanged a fue broadesides the ship borded
us upon our larbord quorter by running hour
bowsprit over our quorlad deck our
People that wor staſined upon the quoter
deck all left it exsept 7 of us who
ware determened to dye before wee
wold give up the innomy seing our men
leave the quorterdeck ran forward
with thar spears and tomehakes but
Didnot bring thare smol arm nor
pistorls which wor very luckely for
us that wor on the quorterdeck for
thay mayte killed every one of us had
thay brote thare smorl arm wee having
our guns loded and a number of more
that ware on the quorterdeck wee
Cheked them and by the Desterylti
of Mr Brolhon the french capten
jumped doun upon the main deck

which she immediately returned. We exchanged a few broadsides. The ship boarded us upon our larboard quarter by running her bowsprit over our quarterdeck. Our people that was stationed upon the quarterdeck all left it except 7 of us who were determined to die before we would give up. The enemy, seeing our men leave the quarterdeck, ran forward with their spears and tomahawks but did not bring their small arms nor pistols, which was very luckily for us that was on the quarterdeck for they might killed everyone of us had they brought their small arms. We having our guns loaded and a number of more that were on the quarterdeck, we checked them and by the dexterity of Mr. Proshon, the French captain, jumped down upon the main deck and drove up the men. They were grappled to us for a glass.[10] The action very bloody for that time. We both fought with small arms, blunderbusses, hand grenades, fire flasks, spears and tomahawks, and coehorns out of our tops, then fell off from one another and then played with cannon and small arms. We had engaged about 4 glasses. She hauled down her British colors. We left off firing and gave three cheers and ordered her to hoist out her boat and come on board. We were both of our boats as well as rigging cut almost to bits and we lay alongside

And drove up the men thay ware
Grappled to us for a glas and the
action very bludely for that tyme
wee both fote with small arms
blunderbuſhes hand grannades
fyre flaſkes spears & tome hooks
And couhorns oute of our tops then
fel of from one another and then plaid
with cannon and small arm wee ha
Ingage about 4 glaſses she holled
Down her Britiſh cullors wee left
of fyring and gave three chears and
ordred her to hiſt out her bote and
Come on bord wee ware both of our
boles tote as well as rigging cut
almoſt to bits and wee lay along syde

13   1   7

one another lyke a hulkes wee cold
not make our bote swim nor she
hers before wee cold git a bord her
An 8 gun brig came up under british
Cullors which the ship spred her
Cullors uppon her tassel they both
                                    smart
Ingage us the brig having tite mettol
she wold not cum a long side so that
wee cold give her a brodeside but
Played of a starn and hed which
Raked us the ship a us cep with in
Pirstol shot of one another wee all
morst sillensed her guns again and
Expected every moment when she
wold strike a gen our brave
Commandelr Mr Croshore fel
that brave man had jest come up
of the main deck whare he had

one another like two hulks. We could not make our boat swim nor she hers. Before we could get aboard her an 8 gun brig came up under British colors which the ship spread her colors upon her taffrail. They both engaged us. The brig having small metal she would not come alongside so that we could give her a broadside but played off astern and [a]head which raked us. The ship & us kept within pistol shot of one another. We almost silenced her guns again and expected every moment when she would strike again. Our brave Commander, Mr. Proshon, fell. That brave man had just come off the main deck where he had been encouraging his men. He came to me as I stood to the wheel upon the quarterdeck and seemed to be much pleased that I was not hurt as there was not a man astanding upon the quarterdeck but myself. And I had steered her for 5 glasses. There was 3 men killed to the wheel before I took it. That instant as he stood by me and seemed to be in the height of his glory a cannon ball struck off the top of his head. As soon as the people on the main deck found out that he was dead, they all cried "Haul down the colors" and unlaid the hatches and one half of them were in the hold before they had time

then incurriging his men he came
to me as I stud to the wheal upon
the quorterdeck and semed to be much
much pleassed that I worr not hort
As thare worr not a man a standing
upon the quorterdeck but myself
And I had steared hor for y glasses
thare worr 3 men killed to the wheal
before I tuck it that instant as he
stud by me and semed to be in the hath
of his glory a cannon bole struck
of the top of his hed as sun as the
People on the main deck found out
that he wors ded thay all cryed hol
Down the cullors and onlaid the
haches and one half of them wore
in the hole before thay had tyme

to hal down the cullors the hole
Ingagement laasted 7 glasses and
all the tyme within pistol shot
Wee had 100 men including offesers
And Boys when the ingagement begun
wee had bter then half killed and
wounded the Orstreg had 120 men
And had all hor offesers killed
and mortolle wounded and above half
of hor men the Brig that came in
to the asinstance of the ship wors
the Loftaffs tendor Lut Hibs too
too Commandor who came along
tide Syor then he had bin at the
tyme of ingagement after our
Cullors ware struck and gave on
Chear and fyred a brode tide at us
And ordered us to hist out our bote
And cum abord him we told him

to haul down the colors. The whole engagement lasted 7 glasses and all the time within pistol shot. We had 100 men including officers and boys when the engagement begun. We had better than half killed and wounded. The *Ostrich* had 120 men and had all her officers killed and mortally wounded and above half of her men. The brig that came up to the assistance of the ship was the *Lostafs*, [*Lowestoffe's Prize*] tender, Lieut. Hibbs, Commander, who came alongside, nigher than he had been at the time of engagement after our colors were struck and gave one cheer and fired a broadside at us and ordered us to hoist out our boat and come aboard him. We told him that our boat was stove. He hoisted out his boat and came aboard and called for the Capt. I told him that he was dead. He asked for the First Lieutenant. "He is dead." He asked for the Second Lieut. I told him he was not dead but mortally wounded, as I thought. Then said he, "What Officer are you, you damned rascal?" I told him that I was a passenger aboard. He told me if I did not get the papers in a moment he would run me through with his sword and asked, "Where's the Capt. sword?" I told him that I believed that it twas somewhere upon deck. He seemed to be in such an agony and still threatening to put us all to death I could not tell what he wanted. I told him that I would find the Clerk

that our bote wors stove he hifted
out his bote and came a bord and
Colled for the Capt I told him that
he wors ded he asked for the furst
Leutennont he is ded he asked for the
hechont Lieut I told him he wors not
ded but mortolly wounded as I thote
then said he whot offessior are you
you Damd rashorl I told him that
I wors a passioncser a bord he told
me if I didnot get the peequors in a
moment hewold run me thru with
his sword and asked whair's the Capt
I word I told him that I beleave
that it twors sum whare ugion decke
he semed to be in thuch anaggony and
stil threlneng to put us all to deth
I cold not tel whot he wonted I
told him that I wold fynd the Clark

9

And git the peapors accordingly
I did he cared the Clark and pragm
a bord the shipe thay cared him of
our wounded a bord the shipe and
the Doctor part of the well men
men he caryed a bord his brig and
ordred the pryse marster to put the
rest Doun the hole. I worr slitely
wounded by the forr of a cannon bord
one arm and one thy wheck swelled
arich which the pryse marster let
me lye upon the deck with some more
wounded John Buckland worr slitle
Wounded on both legs which thay
Caryed him a bord the shipe to be
Dresed I sharnt doe Buckland
justes with out I menchon hiss
behaaure in tyme of action
at the tyme the shipe attampted

and get the papers. Accordingly I did. He carried the Clerk and papers aboard the ship. They carried some of our wounded aboard the ship and the Doctor. Part of the well men . . . he carried aboard his brig and ordered the prize master to put the rest down the hold. I was slightly wounded by the force of a cannon ball, one arm and one thigh which swelled much, which the prize master let me lie upon the deck with some more wounded. John Buckland was slightly wounded on both legs which they carried him aboard the ship to be dressed. I shan't do Buckland justice without I mention his behavior in time of action. At the time the ship attempted to board us he was the first man of the main deck upon the quarterdeck and took up a blunderbuss and fought with an undaunted spirit notwithstanding he was wounded in one of his legs, and while he was afighting upon the quarterdeck a fire flask fell so nigh him that burnt one, the other, leg very bad. He never left his quarters and after the ship fell off from us, he went to the gun that he was stationed where was 3 more Americans, which was all the Americans that was aboard except myself. That gun was fought the best aboard. I stayed aboard very quiet until the next day. Lieut. Hibbs, the Capt. of the brig, came aboard,

to bord us he wors the furst man
of the maindeck upon the quorterdeck
And tuck up a blunderbufs and
fote with an undanted speavet
woturthstanding he wors werunded in
one of his legs and while he wors a
fyting upon the quorterdeck a fyer
flafk fel so nye him that burnt
one the other leg very bad he
never left his quorters and after
the ship fel of from us he went
to the gune that he wors flafkoned
whare wors 3 more amaracans which
wors all the amaracans that wors a
bord escept my self that gune
wors fole the best a bord ————

I stade a bord very quiort until
the next Day Capt Hibs the
Capt of the Brig came a bord

10

Colled me up to him and told me
that I wors a Damd villin and said
Dident you say that you wors nothing
but a pasonger a bord and drue out
his sword and said he I will run you
thru God Dam you I asked him
whether he wors a going to take
my lyfe a way in cowl blud I
told him that I wors in his power
As I wors his prisner Dam you one
Cros luck or If you speak a word
I will run you thru I didnot speak
nor luck at him he struck me in
the focs with his fist which made
the blud run into my mouth as
farst as I cold spit it out he
told me to get into his bote for
he wors a going to cary me a bord
to flog me I tuck up my cloes

called me up to him and told me that I was a damned villain and said, "Did not you say that you was nothing but a passenger aboard?" and drew out his sword and, said he, "I will run you through, God damn you." I asked him whether he was agoing to take my life away in cold blood. I told him that I was in his power as I was his prisoner. "Damn you. One cross look or if you speak a word I will run you through." I did not speak nor look at him. He struck me in the jaw with his fist which made the blood run into my mouth as fast as I could spit it out. He told me to get into his boat for he was agoing to carry me aboard to flog me. I took up some clothes that I had tied up in a handkerchief. He told me that if I carried anything aboard he would put me to death. He carried me aboard. He spoke to his quartermaster. "Tie that damned villain up and give him 39 and put it on well or I put it on to you." The quartermaster got a cord to tie me up. The Capt. looked at me. "O you d[amned] rebel, what have you to say for yourself?" I told him that I [had] told him that I was his prisoner and could say nothing else. He told the quartermaster to not flog me then but, "Tie him up forward with his hands behind him. And draw his hands up taut to that ringbolt," which was about two feet from the deck.

that I had teyed up in a hand
dercheaf he told me if that I
Caryed any thing a burd he wold
put me to deth he caysed me a bort
He spoke to his quorter marster
Tye that Damd villing up and give
Him 39 and put it on well or I put
It on to you the quorter marster
got a cord to tye me up the capt
luked at me o you I Rebbel
whot have you to say for your
self I told him that I told him that
I wos his prisnor and I cotd say noth
ing els he told the quorter marster
to not flog me then but tye him
up ferrod with his hands behind him
And drew his hands up torte to Stot
Ringbolt which wors a berit two
feat from the deck

It worse two hye for me when I set
Down soe that it dru my up so hye
behind me that it gave me as much
payn as drowing a twoth he cep me
In that condishon about 2 hour.
while I worr in that condishon a
sconer worr a standing torwords
thay tuck hor to be an amarcean
Pryviteer the Lutnnot came to me
And asked me if I wold fyte if he
wold ontye me I told him i woldnot
then he told me I shold be shot. I
told him if he had any felings
for a man in Destrss he wold run
me thru the hart to pit me out
of massorry for that worr all I
Desired of him then the sconer came
up with us she proved to be

It was too high for me when I set down so that it drew me up so high behind me that it gave me as much pain as drawing a tooth. He kept me in that condition about 2 hour. While I was in that condition a schooner was a-standing towards. They took her to be an American privateer. The lieutenant came to me and asked me if I would fight if he would untie me. I told him I would not. Then he told me I should be shot. I told him if he had any feelings for a man in distress he would run me through the heart to put me out of misery for that was all I desired of him. Then the schooner came up with us. She proved to be

one of their cruisers. Then I lamented my hard fortune
that same ball that killed Capt. Proshon did not miss him
and kill me. He kept me in that position for two hours.
Then he spoke to the quartermaster and told him to "bring
that damned rascal" to him. He came and loosed my hands
and took me aft to him. My arms was so strained that I
could not get my hand to my head to pull off my hat.
When I came up to him he spoke to me, "You damned villain, how dare you to come before me with your hat on?"
I made the second attempt to pull off my hat. With a great
deal of difficulty got it off. "O you damned rebel, what
have you got to say for yourself?" says hc. I told him I
could say nothing. "Put that damned scoundrel into the
hold and don't let him

one of thair cressers then I lemented
my hard forten that saim bole that
Killed Capt Proshon didnot mis
him and kil me he cep me in posseshon
for two hours then he spoke to the
Quortermaster and told him to bring
that Damd rascorl to him he come and
Losd my hands and tuck me crost to
him my arms wors so straind that I
cold not git my hand to my hed to
pul of my hat when I came up to
him he spoke to me you damd villin
how dare you to come before me with
your hat on I made the sechond attemp
to pul of my hat with a grate deal of
diffoilkelty got it of you dam reb
ble whot have you got to say for
yourself sase he I told him I hold
say nothing put that Dam scoundyl
into the hole and dont let him

Ney Daylyte thay put me in to the hole
whair won 20 frenchmen and as hot a
Place as ever I won in thay cepe the
hatches layd over all but about
a foot the lenght of the hatch way
the Next day wee got into Mon
tego bay and after wee got in thay
tuck me out and put me in Irons
that wold way about 100 wait
And cep me in for two Days and
nyts thay put me in the hole with
Irons on he wold not suffer me
to stay upon deck nor pull the
Irons of while I won in the hole
And then sent me a shore to gail
thay tuck all my clos from me
and I goes in harde mony and 80
Dollors in paper mony I went a
shore with nothing but a Short
and a pare of trousses and

see daylight." They put me into the hold where was 20 Frenchmen and as hot a place as ever I was in. They kept the hatches laid over all but about a foot the length of the hatchway. The next day we got into Montego Bay, and after we got in they took me out and put me in irons that would weigh about 100 weight and kept me in for two days and nights. They put me in the hold with irons on. He would not suffer me to stay upon deck nor pull the irons off while I was in the hold. And then sent me ashore to jail.[11] They took all my clothes from me and 2 Joes[12] in hard money and 80 dollars in paper money. I went ashore with nothing but a shirt and a pair of trousers and an old pair of shoes and a old hat. A few days after, they set us all at our liberty. I found an American, Mr. Johnson,[13] who invited me to his house and gave me a suit of clothes. I stayed at his house until the 1th of August. Then I went aboard of a sloop [*Active*] bound to New York. I left John Buckland in the hospital. He had not got well of his lameness. There was a sloop [*Independence*] there . . . bound to Rhode Island, Capt. Edmondson, Commander. Israel Fox and John Buckland were agoing home in her. One Mr. Hambottom made me a present of a half Joe which I gave half of it to Buckland and Fox. I agreed with Johnson to let two men to have anything they wanted and I would see him paid.

An old pare of shoes and a old
hat a few Days after thay set
us all at our libberty & found
an amarakan Mr Johnson who
Invyted me to his house and gave me
a sute of Cloes & stade at his house
Until the 1th of Auguest then
I went a bord of a Sloope bound
to nuyork I left John Buckland
In the horspittol he had not got
well of his lamefress thair wons a
Sloope thar wons a Sloope thair bound
to horsfilland Capt Edmonson
Commander first Jose and Jose
Buckland wair a going home in hor
one Mr Flambotton made me a presont
of a half Joe which I gave half
of It to Buckland and Jose I agreed
with Jonson to Let the two men
to have anything thay wonted
And I wold Ley him pay

15   13

The 5th of August 1779

Went on Bord of the Sloope Active
John Underwood Captn as a hand to
Doe my Duty to work the sloop to New
York Jeams Taylor thwos mait
two inglish ropman & 3 amarchans
that wors prisnors teaken by Capt
Hill in the royel george thair naymes
are Artemos White Aquilla Pearsol
Daved Clark who ware put a bord
By Capt hill as prisnors to work
the vessel to New york thare wors
three gentolmen passongers and
two negros which made 13 of us all
August 8th wee jind the linnon
fleat under Convoy of the Glass
sc a 20 gun ship and two Sloopes
of wor wee Cep Compr with them until
wee got into the Lat 34

Sunday August 30th left the
fleat in Company of two

This 1th of August 1778 went on board of the sloop *Active*, John Underwood, Captain, as a hand to do my duty to work the sloop to New York. James Taylor was mate. Two English seamen and 3 Americans that was prisoners taken by Capt. Hill in the *Royal George*. Their names are Artemas White, Aquila Ramsdell,[14] David Clark, who were put aboard by Capt. Hill as prisoners to work the vessel to New York. There was three gentlemen passengers and two Negroes which made 13 of us all. August 11th we joined the London fleet under convoy of the *Glasgow*, a 20 gun ship, and two sloops of war.[15] We kept company with them until we got into the Ltt [latitude] 34. Sunday, August 30th, left the fleet in company of two sloops that was bound to New York. One of them was from Jamaica that sailed with us. The other was the *Sea-flower* sloop that was taken from me when I was homeward bound from Guadeloupe with a cargo of molasses, coffee, and tea and salt which had been down to the Bay of Honduras with the ship that took her. As there was no court of admiralty the ship was agoing to carry her home to London. She sailed the 28th of June for London in company with the ship. The day that we left the fleet she came into the fleet and was out of water and provisions. She could not get provisions and water enough out of the fleet to last her home. She was obliged to put away for

which were bound to new york

sloopes that wors bound to new york
one of them wors from Jemeca that sail'd
with us the other wors the Seyflour
a sloope that wors taken from me
when I wors homeward bound from
Gaudeloupe with a cargo of molaffes
coffe and teay and salt which had
bin Deun to the bay of honderos
with the ship that tuck her as
thair wors knon cort of admorlty
the ship wors a going to cary her
home to London she sail'd the 28th
of June for London in comp with the
ship the Pay that wee left the
fleat she came into the fleete and
wors out of worter and provisions
she cold not git provishons
and worter a nuf out of the fleet
to larft hor home she wors a
bliged to put away for

Newyork Mr ~~Flemming~~ and Hodg
ware a bord hee saith that wee
taken in her wee in company with
the two sloopes until thursday Sep 5th
and wee them fryday morning about
12 it being squolle wee lorst site
of them at 6 PM saw the land
brauer W which was the Eastern
there of vergine at & spoke with
a perriticear Brig of 16 guess out
of newyork she informed us that
the Brittish trups had left Pha
ledelpha and if wee didnot keepe
well to the Eastward wee thold
be taken which occasiond us to keep
father of the capes then wee shold
had wee not spoke him Satordey
at sun set wee saw the two sloopes
to the westward that ~~left~~ the
fleat when wee did as wee thote
Sunday 6th at 2 PM spoke with

New York. Mr. Deming and Hodge were aboard, the same that was taken in her. We kept company with the two sloops until Thursday Sept. 5th [3d] and saw them Friday morning about 12. It being squally, we lost sight of them. At 6 P.M. saw the land bearing NW which was the Eastern Shore of Virginia. At 8 spoke with a privateer brig of 16 guns out of New York. She informed us that the British troops had left Philadelphia and if we did not keep well to the Eastward we should be taken, which occasioned us to keep further off the capes than we should had we not spoke him. Saturday at sunset we saw the two sloops to the westward that left the fleet when we did, as we thought. Sunday, 6th, at 2 P.M. spoke with a brig out of New York called the *Tryorl*[16] in latt 38:10. She informed us that the American cruisers was very numerous within shore all along from Egg Harbor to New York and if we kept any further in we should be taken, and if we saw any sail it would most certainly be a Rebel privateer for there was an embargo upon all British cruisers in New York, and he should not get out if he had not been in favor with the Admiral by giving him intelligence of the French fleet. He told Capt. Underwood that he would advise him not to hold in with the land until he got in the latitude of 40 and to make some part of Long Island. The capt. of the brig offered to lend Capt. Underwood two swivels until he got to New York. The capt. told

a Brig out of new york Colled the
Tryort in datt 38:10 she informd
us that the amareton Crucers wars
very numeros within Shore ola long
from Eg harbor to nuey ork and if
wee cep any forther in wee shold
be tachen and if wee sow any sail
It wold morft sertenly be a nebble
Prqurtlear for there wors an inbargo
Upon all Brittish crucers in new
york and he shold not got out if
he had not bin in favor with the
Admorel by giving him inteligencee
of the french fleat he told Capt
Underword that he wold advyse
him not to hole in with the land
Untill he got in the Leitt ofso and
to make some part of Longesland
the Cap of the Breg offred to lend
Cap Unnerword two swarets untill
Se got to new york the Cap told

told him that wee had got two carr[a]dg
Guns and two naivbol guns and he
thote he thote that wors as many us
he had men to fyte the people that
came a bord us from the Brig told
us that the men of wor presed all
the saylors that come in wee asked
them whether thay pressed amarchens
thay told us that it made know ods
whot cuntramen thay wors for thay
pressed all which I thote wee wold
try to disscuring them of having
Amarchens in thain sarvis the
Brig sted to the southwrrd
then wa went to fising our guns
In order to keeep of smoll craft
a cording to the Captens orders
George hoblords an inglishmon
said if thees yankhees dont
fyte thay wold turn the guns

. . . him that we had got two carriage guns and two swivel guns and he thought . . . that was as many as he had men to fight. The people that came aboard us from the brig told us that the men of war pressed all the sailors that came in. We asked them whether they pressed Americans. They told us that it made no odds what countrymen they was for they pressed all, which I thought we would try to discourage them of having Americans in their service. The brig stood to the southward. Then we went to fixing our guns in order to keep off the small crafts according to the Captain's orders. George Roberts, an Englishman, said if these Yankees don't fight they would turn the guns upon them. From 8 to 12 the starboard watch was upon deck. The Capt. was below in the cabin. Robert Robson, Aquila Ramsdell, and myself were upon deck as we were in the starboard watch. At 11 Ramsdell called up Artemas White & David Clark, and four of us agreed to take the sloop from the captain and others and carry her into Egg Harbor.[17] The three that were concerned with me was Artemas White, Aquila Ramsdell, & David Clark and to do it by confining the Capt., mate, and passengers in the cabin and to keep Robert Robson and George Roberts on deck and a Negro that was

upon them from & He is the
Starbord watch was upon deck
the Capt was beloe in the cabben
Robbert Robson Agavillor
Ramsdel and myself were upon
Deck as wee were in the Stearbord
watch at 11 Ramsdell colld up
Artemos While & Dewed Clark
And fore of us agreed to teake
the sloope from the Capt and
others and Cary hor onto Egharbor
the three that ware consarned with
me war Artemos While Agvillar
Ramsdell & Dewed Clark and
to Doe it by Confyning the
Capt Mate and passengers in
the Cabben and to keeape Robert
Robson and George Robberts on
Deck and a negro that was

a sleep in the fore hole and to doe
It att 12 at nite Sweed Clash went
Below that thay myte not mestrupt
whot our Desine wors and as soon
as wee Colled the wotch at 12 to
Come up and to waich George Robbon
In the mean while wee wors to git
Every ~~comey~~ Insttorement to Deffend
our selves if thay shold make
Any resystence wee got two or 3
Axses and a Crowbar at hand
and teft before wee Colled the wotch
wee Colled up the Negro that wars
forrod and fasned down the scuttot
And told him to keep forrod for
wee shold not hort him and
And told him not to speak a word
at 12 wee Colled the wotch Clash
And George Robborts come up as
sun as thay came up wee holled up
the Laddor and went to quisting

asleep in the forehold and to do it at 12 at night. David Clark went below that they might not mistrust what our design was and as soon as we called the watch at 12 to come up and to wake George Roberts. In the meanwhile we was to get every instrument to defend ourselves if they should make any resistance. We got two or 3 axes and a crowbar at hand and just before we called the watch we called up the Negro that was forward and fastened down the scuttle and told him to keep forward, for we should not hurt him, and told him not to speak a word. At 12 we called the watch. Clark and George Roberts came up. As soon as they came up we hauled up the ladder and went to coiling a cable over the companionway. As soon as Robson and Roberts saw what we were about . . . they begged that we would not hurt them. We told them that we would not if they would be peaceable. They told us that they would. We told Robson to take the helm and steer. We had coiled so much of the cable before they found it out they could not get out though they made several attempts. We secured them down and jibed the boom and steered NW with a pleasant breeze. A few moments after, there was a pistol shot out of the cabin and hit me upon my thigh but did not enter the flesh. By that I knew that it was not a bullet. And we thought they had none in the cabin as we had a large bag of musket balls on deck that we had brought up the day before and thought

a Cabol over the Companeun way
As sun as frobberson and roberts
hers that thay beges that wee wold
not hort them wee told them that
wee wold not if thay wold be peac
ble thay told us that thay wold
wee told frobberson to take the
Helm and stear wee had opurled
so much of the Cable before thay
found it out thay cold not go too
tho thay made owrel otenpus
wee secured them Down and jibed
the boome and stearde NW with
a pleasont breas a fue moments after
there worr a pistol shot out of the
Cabeen and hit me upon my thy but
dident enter the flesh by that so I
knew that it warnot a buflit
And wee thot thay had none in the
Cabeen as wee had a large bac of
Mushkil bolts on deck tha wee had
borte up the day before and thort

them wors all thare wors a bord wee
wee had to Cartorges of pouder for the
Cannon and 8 or 10 for the swivels
And a large horn full wee had a
number of Cannon bols on deck
wee poynted the guns aft and told
them if thay fired out a gain wee
wold fire into the cabben thay fyred
once or twice but did not hurt anybody
wee thot it a pesty to kil them tho
wee kold doe it several tymes as
thay put thair heds out of the
Cabben windows to try to shoot us
thay told us that if wee wold let
them cume up thay wold yous us well
And wold set us a shore on longisland
I told them that I had bin deceaved by
the Brittish party and wold not truft
won of them thare wors not mutch done
after that that night at day lyte
A monday morning thay began to

them was all there was aboard. We . . . had 6[?] cartridges of powder for the cannon and 8 or 10 for the swivels and a large hornful. We had a number of cannon balls on deck. We pointed the guns aft and told them if they fired out again we would fire into the cabin. They fired once or twice but did not hurt anybody. We thought it a pity to kill them though we could do it several times as they put their heads out of the cabin windows to try to shoot us. They told us that if we would let them come up they would use us well and would set us ashore on Long Island. I told them that I had been deceived by the British party and would not trust none of them. There was not much done after that that night. At daylight a Monday morning they began to fire out of the cabin as they could see through betwixt the cable. They wounded David Clark in the thigh and slightly wounded me. We fired two 4 pounders through the bulkhead into the cabin and . . . unbent our foresail and covered them up so that they could not see out which put a stop to their firing. Then they wedged up our rudder. We told them that it did not trouble us at all their wedging the rudder for we could steer her as it was; and we was not concerned about being taken by their cruisers for we was sure we was out of the way of them; and we had got provisions and water enough as we had a half dozen sheep and goats and two coops of fowls and ducks, two live turtles, and one that we had killed, and a barrel of corn, a barrel of [?],

fyer out of the Cabben as thay cold
tey thay beturel the Cable thay woundd
fare blash in the ley and thylole wound
me wee fyred two 4 pounders thay the
bulk hed into the Cabben and
And onbent our forefail and hisred
them up soe that thay coldnot tey
out which put a stop to thair
fyring then thay urged up our ruddor
wee told them that it didnot
trubbol us at tol thare urging
the ruddor for wee cold stear her
as it wors and wee wors not confarned
About being teaken by thare
Cruesers for wee wors shure wee
wors out of the way of them and
wee had got provissions and wrted
A nuf as wee had a half a duefore
sheepe and gotes and two koopes of
fouls and duks two wyee bunlols
And one that wee had killed and
a barel of Corne a barel of   18

And about 20 gallons of water
In our fore hole thay Cut a hole out
of the compannen way so that thay
Cold sea out wee quet in the
Nessol of a swivel that wors lorde
with ~~grast the~~ musket boles
which jest fillid up the hole
~~thay~~ then wee told them that wee
wors a going to onway the rudder
And if thay offred to cut any more
holes or did any thing to hurt us
wee would fier into the cabbes
with the swivel that wors pinted
Down wee went to wocking away
the plank of the stern to come
at the wegges thay seamed to bee
uppon sum merement in the cabbes
wee fyred down into the cabben with
the swivel that wors pinted for that

and about 20 gallons of water. In our forehold they cut a hole out of the companionway so that they could see out. We put in the muzzle of a swivel that was loaded with musket balls which just filled up the hole. Then we told them that we was agoing to unwedge the rudder and if they offered to cut any more holes or did anything to hurt us, we would fire into the cabin with the swivel that was pointed down. We went to knocking away the plank of the stern to come at the wedges. They seemed to be upon some movement in the cabin. We fired down into the cabin with the swivel that was pointed for that design which they had to put their heads out of the cabin windows to breathe which we could easily put them to death if we had been a mind to. They asked us what we meant, whether we meant to kill them or not. We told them we would not hurt them if they would be peaceable below. We loaded our swivel and put it in the same place it was before and went to knocking away the stern. Mr. [Robert] Jackson and Mr. [James] Holmes told us that if we would be easy a few moments they would try to prevail with Capt. Underwood to unwedge the rudder. We left off knocking away the stern. They unwedged the rudder. It was then about 12 o'clock A.M. We had a pleasant breeze at the southward in 35 fathom of water and off Egg Harbor by

Desire which thay had to put thair
Heds out of the Cabben windoes to
Breath which wee cold easaly put
them to deth if wee had bin a mynd
to thay asked us whot wee ment
whether wee ment to kil them or
not wee told them wee wold not
hurt them if thay wold be pease
ble bele wee loded our wiliams
put it in the saim place it wors
before and went to nocking a way
the sturn Mr Jackson and Mr Homes
told us that if wee wold be easy a
fue moments thay wold try to pro
veal with Capt Underwood to on
wag the ruddor wee left of nock
ind away the sturn thay onwaged the
ruddor it wors then about 12 a
Clok at Nit wee had a pleasont
Breas at the Southward in 35 fathom
of worter and of Edghorbor by 19

our tendance we cept hor ew W
thay asked us if wee wold heich
them a forel wee told them that
wee had heiched non mutton that
Day and thay myte have sum of
that thay told us that thay
wold be ablige to us for sum of
that wee gave them a leg of mutton
over the stoarn into the Cabben win
dores thay Didnot make any defterbance
to the Cabben at wenderin wee wore
in 23 fathom of worter wee had a
pleafont Breeas all nite at
Daylite wee wore in 13 fathom
of worter wee sow a sail Bare NW
wee holled Down all sail to wotch
hor motion at sun rife wee sow the
land Baring as the sail did wee
hold not tel which way the

our soundance. We kept her NW. They asked us if we would cook them a fowl. We told them that we had cooked some mutton that day and they might have some of that. They told us that they would be obliged to us for some of that. We gave them a leg of mutton over the stern into the cabin windows. They did not make any disturbance in the cabin. At sundown we was in 23 fathom of water. We had a pleasant breeze all night. At daylight we were in 13 fathom of water. We saw a sail bearing NW. We hauled down all sail to watch her motion. At sunrise [September 8] we saw the land bearing as the sail did. We could not tell which way the sail was standing. We thought if she proved to be a British sail and [we] was obliged to put to sea to get out of her way, we should not have more water than to last us 6 days. We thought we would try to take the strength out of rum, as we did by burning it. We burned it as long as it would burn and let it stand in the air until got cold. It was as weak as grog. This sail stood out by the wind until she bore west of us. We could see that she was a brig. We made all sail and steered North. As soon as we made sail the brig hove about and stood athwart us. She looked ahead of us. By that we thought she was a British cruiser as she seemed to try to cut us

sail wors standing wee thote if she
proved to be a Brittish sail and wors
a bliged to put to sey to git out
of hor way wee shold not have
more worter then to hoyst us 6
Days wee thote wee wold try to
take the strenght out of rum
as wee did By Bernning it wee
burnt it as long as it wold burn
And let it stand in the are until
got cold it wors as weeak as
grog this sail steid out by the wine
Until she bore west of us wee cold
sey that she wors a Brig wee made
All sail and steard worth as
nen as wee made sayl the Brig
hove a boul and steid a hole us
she luked a hed of us by that wee
thote she wors a Brittish conceor
as she seamed to try to cut us

34   20

of from the Land wee ware with in
three leags of the land the brig
fyred a gun under brittish cullor
the shot went jest a starn of us
wee holled down owr squairsale
And brole owr vessel tw the Brig
Run along side of us and hailled
us she asked us whare wee wiis from
from wee told them wee wors from
Jamece thay asked us whare wee wis
Bound wee told them Egharbor
then thay holled down thare brittiss
Cullors and hifted Continentel
Cullors and asked us whot sloope
wee wors wee told them she wors
A pryse teakon from Capt
Hue Underwood by his laymes
Jasked whot Brig that wors

off from the land. We were within three leagues of the land. The brig fired a gun under British colors. The shot went just astern of us. We hauled down our square sail and brought our vessel to. The brig run alongside of us and hailed us. She asked us where we was from. We told them we was from Jamaica. They asked us where we was bound. We told them Egg Harbor. Then they hauled down their British colors and hoisted Continental colors and asked us what sloop we was. We told them she was a prize taken from Capt. John Underwood by his seamen. I asked what brig that was.

He said it was the *Convention* belonging to the state of Pennsylvania, Thomas Houston, commander. He hoisted out his boat and sent his Lieutenant aboard. He asked where our papers was. I told him the papers and prisoners were all confined in the cabin, and we did not intend to let them out before we got into port. The Lieutenant told the Captain what we said. The Captain told him to send me aboard. I told the Capt. we did not want any of his assistance. The Lieutenant told me to go aboard in their boat. I went aboard. The Capt. asked me whether we had seen any vessels lately.

He said it wors the Convenxion
Belonging to the state of Pencelvany
Thommos Horston Commanden
He hirstes out his bote and
sent his Lutennont a bord he
Asked whare our papors wors I
told him the peapors and prisnors
ware all confynd in the Cabben
And wee didnot intend to let
them out before wee got into port
the Lutennont told the Capten
whot wee said the Capten told
him to send me a bord I told
the Capt wee didnot wornt
Any of his asistence the
Lutennont told me to goe a bord
In thare bote I went a bord the
Capt asked me wheather wee had
ban any vessels lately

I told him him the large wee sow
wor a Brig out of newyork the sunday
before and she told us that thare
wos know brittish Crucers out
of newyorke a loud to come out
And thare wor none a Cruciend of
that shore I told him thayr wor
two sloopes that left the fleat
when wee did but parted with
us thre or fore days before and
thay wor sumewhare nye the capes
As thay hadnot heard of the brit
tish troups leaving Phaledelfa
thay intended to keeap very nye
he asked whather thay wor both
from jemeco I told him one wor
the other wor a sloope that wor
teahen from me and a good cargo
in of Molasses and dry goods

I told him the last we saw was a brig out of New York the Sunday before, and she told us that there was no British cruisers out of New York allowed to come out. And there was none acruising off that shore. I told him there was two sloops that left the fleet when we did but parted with us three or four days before and they was somewhere near the capes. As they had not heard of the British troops leaving Philadelphia they intended to keep very nigh. He asked whether they was both from Jamaica. I told him one was; the other was a sloop that was taken from me and a good cargo in of molasses and dry goods and had been carried to the Bay of Honduras but was then bound to New York. He asked whether they had any guns aboard. I told him they had none except the sloop that was taken from me. She had four swivels. I asked him whether he did not intend to put away after them. He said that he was agoing to carry us to Philadelphia. I told him we could carry her ourselves either to Philadelphia or to Egg Harbor. He said that we had no commission and he should make a prize of her. I told him I thought the state of Pennsylvania would not thank him for bringing in vessels that was acoming in themselves. He said that he should do as he pleased.

And had bin Carryed to the Bay
of honderes, but was then bound
to New york he asked wheather thay
had any guns aberd I told him
thay had none except the sloope that
was teahon from me she had three
swivels I asked him wheather
He Rdnot intend to quit a way
After them he said that he was
a going to Cary us to phaledefpha
I told him wee Cold cary hor our
selves ither to phaledelfia or to
Egharber he said that wee had
know Comission and he shold work
a pryse of hor I told him I
hole the State of Pencolveney
wold not thank him for bringng
In vesels that wors a comming
In thare selves he said that
he shold doe as he pleafed

It wors then a bout one a Clok
He broke open the Cobben and
taich out Capt and ga and other
pasnors In a bout 2 hores after
Wee got into the Dellowware rivers
wee ran up a littlle ways and
Came two the Brig herfled out
flor bote to Cary Capt Underwo
And the other passengers a bord the
Sloope I asked the Capt If he wold
let me goe a bord he told me he
hold not let me goe then I told
him that I had know cloes thair
but a short and a pear of
trowfes that I had on and It
wors very Cold he told me I
Muerſt take sum other tyme
for I Cold not goe with them
gentolmen Cap Huerſson went
a bord with the gento men as
he colled them

44/

It was then about one o'clock. He broke open the cabin and took out Capt. and other prisoners. In about 2 hours after we got into the Delaware River we ran up a little ways and came to. The brig hoisted out her boat to carry Capt. Underwood and the other passengers aboard the sloop. I asked the Capt. if he would let me go aboard. He told me he could not let me go. Then I told him that I had no clothes there but a shirt and a pair of trousers that I had on and it was very cold. He told me I must take some other time for I could not go with them gentlemen. Capt. Houston went aboard with the gentlemen, as he called them, and brought White, Ramsdell and Clark aboard. After they came aboard they asked me what they was agoing to do with us. I told them I did not know. I asked what the Capt. of the brig told them. They said all the Capt. said was he told his people to carry them pirates aboard of the brig. He kept us aboard that night. We was obliged to lie in the hold among a passel [of] people that was very lousy. The next day we got up within 10 or twelve miles of Reedy Island[18] and came to, this being Wednesday and very cold and stormy. At night it cleared off but cold. We told the Captain that we thought very hard that he kept us aboard and would not suffer us

And brote White from sidol and
Clork a bord after thay Came a
bord thay asked me whot thay wors a
going to doe with us I told them
I dednot know I asked whot the
Capt of the Brig told them thay
had all the Capt said wors he told
his people to Cary them Reyools
a Bord of the Brig he cep us a
bord that nyte ther wors a bleged
to lye in the hole a mong a perfsol
people that wors vary lousse the
next day wee got up within soon
twelve miles of reole Island and
Came tes this Being wednsoday
And very Cold and storme at
nite it cleared of but cold
wee told the Copten that wee
frote very harde that he cep
us a bord and wold not seffer us

to git a shift of cloes from the
sloope to put on theurdsday we
got up as far as headeestand I
who one of the offesors who wors the
treafor the Capt Confyneing us
a bord and yourfeind Capt Andsourou
and the passongers wors alowed all
the liborty that any jentolmen
wonted as then he wors a rowing
them a shore with thair beft
cloes on and wee wors not aloued
to come at our cloes the the beft
of myne wors bad a nuf for when
I wors teahore by them I had all
my cloes teahore from me and
yf I hadnot found an amarchan
that made me a prefont of
a sute of cloes I shold not have
any then but as I had them I thote
harde that he woldnot let me

to get a shift of clothes from the sloop to put on.
Thursday we got up as far as Reedy Island. I asked one of
the officers what was the reason the captain confining us
aboard and using [us] so. Capt. Underwood and the passengers was allowed all the liberty that any gentleman
wanted as then he was arowing them ashore with their
best clothes on, and we was not allowed to come at our
clothes though the best of mine was bad enough, for when
I was taken by them I had all my clothes taken from me.
And if I had not found an American that made me a
present of a suit of clothes I should not have any then. But
as I had them, I thought hard that he would not let me

go aboard the sloop and get them, for I had got very lousy since we came aboard him. I asked him what Capt. Houston was agoing to do with us. He said that he heard him say that he was agoing to carry us out to sea. I told him that we should be no profit to him if he carried us out. He said that he would set us ashore at Egg Harbor. I told him that we chose to be set ashore there or go up in the sloop. Before the night the Capt. told us that we might go up in the sloop but must not say nothing to the gentle-men nor go below, for if we did they swore they would shoot us. He carried us aboard the sloop the next day, which was Friday, the 11th.

goe a bord the sloope and get them
for I had got very loufse sence
wee came a bord him I afhed him
whot Capt Steurfton woos a going
to doe with us he said that he heard
him say that he woos a going
to Cary us out to sey I told
him that wee shold be know
proffit to him if he Carid us out
he said that he wold set us a shore
at Ey harbor I told him that
wee choos to be set a shore thair
or goe up in the sloope before the
night the Capt told us that
wee myght goe up in the sloope
but must not say nothing to
the gentolman nor goe belec for
If wee did thay swore thay wold
thut us he C009ed us a bord the
sloope the next Day which
wos fryday the 11th

Capt Slouson come a bord of the sloop
And tuck out all the cabben forneteur
he tuck out 2 barels of beeaf and a
barel of rum and sundre other things of
value a chest of meaderfons and a
half a barel of pouder he gave the
Prise marfter orders not to alow ani of
us to goe beloe nor to goe a shore
Except the gentelmen as he colled
them but wee coll them prifnors
Saterday morning wee got up as
far as Chester the bote wos a going
a shore I got into the bote and wea
a shore and set of for Pheladelfa
a fut I got to the sitle little before
wee went to Mager Ginnorel
Arnort and told him how I was
yoused By Capt Slouston and that
we had know frinds that wee nere
of nor know money he told me that

Capt. Houston came aboard of the sloop and took out all the cabin furniture. He took out 2 barrels of beef and a barrel of rum and sundry other things of value, a chest of medicines and a half a barrel of powder. He gave the prize master orders not to allow any of us to go below nor to go ashore except the gentlemen, as he called them but we called them prisoners. Saturday morning we got up as far as Chester. The boat was agoing ashore. I got into the boat and went ashore and set off for Philadelphia afoot. I got to the city little before night. I went to Major General [Benedict] Arnold[19] and told him how I was used by Capt. Houston and that we had no friends that we knew of nor no money. He told me that we should not lose our right for the want of money and if it was as I told the story, by the laws of the Congress the prize belonged to us. A Sunday morning the sloop got up to the town and lay off in the stream. I went aboard to see the rest of my shipmates and told them that we would go ashore. The man that had the command told us that their committee had been aboard and left orders that we should none of us go ashore. The next morning they hauled alongside of the wharf and allowed us to go ashore. We went ashore and libeled the sloop in our names. She was tried before the Court of Admiralty the last of October, George Ross,[20] Judge. The Court gave us one quarter

wee shold not lose our veyte for the
want of mony and If it wer as I told
the story by the foes of the Congris the
Pryes belonged to us a sunday morning
the sloope got up to the toun and lay
of in the stream I went a bord to sey
the rest of my ship mates and told
them that wee wold goe a shore the
mean that had the Command told us
that their Committe had bin a bord
And left orders that wee shold
sume of us goe a shore the next
mornning thay holled a long side
of the worf and a bord us to goe
a shore wee went a shore and
by bild the sloope in our names
Our She wars tryed before the
Cort of Admoralty the lorst of
october George howes judg the Co
Gave us one Quorter

And the other three Quarters to
the Brig Convention and a Sloope
that wars In sile when the Brig
Came on bird us Capt Jobson
wars Commander of the Sloope
Wee apeard from that Cort
To the Congress December the 18
It wars tryed before the Cort
thay Gave the Hole to us
And Gave orders to judg
Tross to order the Money to
be payd to the judg Tross
Got all the mony into his
Hands and refused to pay us
all the reason he geve wars
that the Congress had hear
rule to Give all he had

and the other three quarters to the brig *Convention* and a sloop [*Le Gerard*] that was in sight when the brig came on board us. Capt. [James] Josiah was Commander of the sloop. We appealed from that Court to the Congress December 18th. It was tried before the Congress. They gave the whole to us and gave orders to Judge Ross to order the money to be paid to us. Judge Ross got all the money into his hands and refused to pay us. All the reason he gave was that the Congress had no right to try a case that had [been settled by the Court of Admiralty of Pennsylvania].[21]

NOTES

[1] Gideon Olmsted was described by Connecticut Governor Jonathan Trumbull in 1782 as "33 years of age, 5 feet 10 inches high, grey eyes, light coloured long hair, light complexion, middling sett." At the same time Trumbull described Israel Deming as "32 years of age, six feet two inches high—grey eyes, light coloured short hair, light complexion, middling sett–round shoulders." Endorsement to Commission granted to Gideon Olmsted, Commander of the *General Green*, printed in Louis F. Middlebrook, *History of Maritime Connecticut During the American Revolution*, vol. 2 (Salem, Mass.: The Essex Institute, 1925), p. 95.

[2] Antony Gernat & Company of Port Louis, located on the coast of Grande Terre, Guadeloupe.

[3] Admiralty court records indicate that the *Seaflower* was captured April 6, 1778, and carried into New York, where she was libeled and condemned on September 21, 1778. Bundle 457, High Court Admiralty, Public Record Office, London, cited in Louis F. Middlebrook, *Captain Gideon Olmsted, Connecticut Privateersman, Revolutionary War* (Salem, Mass.: Newcomb & Gauss Co., 1933), p. 20. See also Olmsted journal, pp. 27 and 28.

[4] Snow: a small sailing vessel resembling a brig, carrying a mainmast, a foremast and a supplementary trysail close behind the mainmast.

[5] Sloop: a small sailing vessel with one mast and often with nothing but fore-and-aft sails, the mainsail being extended by a gaff and a boom and attached to the mast on its foremost edge.

[6] Tender: a small sailing vessel attending a larger one with supplies or used to convey intelligence. The *Niger*, 32 guns and 220 tons, had been sailing in American waters since early in the year.

[7] Schooner: a small seagoing fore-and-aft rigged vessel with two masts, first launched in 1713 in Gloucester, Mass.

[8] Brig: a light sailing vessel with two masts, square rigged. *Polly* was owned by Paul de Verge, a resident of Port-au-Prince, was navigated by a Scotsman, Henry Marchant, and carried a French crew, according to Middlebrook, *Olmsted*, pp. 30–35. Middlebrook makes no mention of Mr. Proshon, but he might be Lieutenant Jacques, who commanded the *Polly* before Olmsted's appointment.

[9] Commanded by Peter Rainier, captain in the British navy.

[10] Time glass: in this and subsequent references, probably half an hour.

[11] Olmsted was imprisoned in the old fort dungeon when the *Lowestoffe's Prize* reached Montego Bay, July 10. Middlebrook, *Olmsted*, pp. 41–48.

[12] Johannes: a Portuguese gold coin issued between 1722 and 1835; a half joe was worth about eight dollars (Spanish) or 1 pound 12 shillings (British), with its value in United States continental dollars fluctuating widely.

[13] This is probably the same Henry Johnson of Jamaica, whose ship, *Mary*, was captured at New Providence in January 1778 by a Rhode Island privateer. See "Journal of Lieutenant John Trevett," *Rhode Island Historical Magazine* 7 (July 1886): 40, 42.

[14] "Ramsdell" is the most likely modern spelling for this name, which has been rendered variously as "Rumsdale" and "Ramsdall" in the sources consulted on the case of the *Active*.

[15] Sloop of war: a small warship, usually armed on a single deck with fewer than 18 guns.

[16] The *Tryon*, Capt. Bridger Goodrich of Bermuda, commanding. See Middlebrook, *Olmsted*, p. 58; also deposition of Robert Robson, in *Sundry Documents*, p. 19, and that of George Roberts, ibid, p. 24.

[17] Just south of present-day Atlantic City, N.J., Egg Harbor was a haven for American privateers during the war.

[18] Reedy Island, 1½ miles long, lies in the Delaware River south of Philadelphia and just east of Port Penn.

[19] Benedict Arnold was military commander in Philadelphia after the British withdrawal in 1778. See note 5 to introduction.

[20] George Ross (1730–79), lawyer and signer of the Declaration of Independence, was commissioned judge of the Pennsylvania Admiralty court in March 1779, although he was acting in that capacity in the fall of 1778 under authority of the revolutionary government.

[21] The last fragment of the manuscript is missing, but this bracketed conclusion was transcribed on the back cover sheet of the journal.

CODA: The Language of Olmsted's Journal

Charles W. Kreidler

FOR ANY READER Captain Olmsted's journal is an absorbing account of a series of adventures. It contains pathos, suspense, exhilaration; above all, it portrays a persistent, "undanted" individual carrying on tirelessly against the misfortunes which befall him. For the reader who studies the manuscript, the "Jurnnorl" is likely to be as striking for the manner of Olmsted's communication as for the matter communicated. The medium, one might say, has a kind of message of its own. We are struck by the variant spellings which the author has for the same word (*fleet, fleat, fleate*), his apparently haphazard way of dividing words (*a state* for *estate*), and the seemingly arbitrary way he has of using capital letters. We cannot help being bewildered or amused, perhaps both, when we find *sofishont* for *sufficient*, *twoth* for *tooth*, or *Pencolvany* as the name of the state in which *Phaledelfa* (or *Phaladefpha* or *Pholedelfa*) is located.

Our reactions are, of course, in us rather than in the document. We of the 20th century approach any piece of writing with the expectation of finding words spelled in the way we have always seen them spelled. We take it for granted that orthography should be consistent, though this is a bit strange if we stop to think about it, for we are accustomed to great variety in other aspects of our language. We know there is a vast reservoir of words from which to choose for anything we want to express, and there are numerous ways of putting words together to form the sentences that express what we want to express. We know that different speakers and writers typically make different choices in the vocabulary and syntax which they use. We take it for granted that language varies according to the people who use it and the situations in which it is used. We do not expect men and women to talk alike, nor teenagers to sound like their grandparents, nor Texans like Rhode Islanders; we find it natural that the language of the courtroom differs from the language of the baseball diamond. We all know that there are two accepted pronunciations of *either* and of *tomato* and of *laboratory*— but we do not believe there should be more than one spelling for each word.

There are, to be sure, some variations in English spelling. British orthography and American differ in some respects, but the differences are not great. The British write *our* in words like *behaviour*, *colour*, and *harbour*, where American English uses just *or*. Britain has *goal*, *kerb*, *syren*, *cheque*, *calibre*, *woollen* where we write *jail*, *curb*, *siren*, *check*, *caliber*, *woolen*. A few more statements and examples like these would suffice for setting out all the spelling differences that exist between the two countries. Then, there are certain spelling variations which the commercial world uses as devices for getting our attention (*Kwik Kleen*, *Kut-ryte*, etc.). Elsewhere nonstandard spellings indicate that the writer is trying to suggest the speech of a particular dialect area (*yalla* for *yellow*, for instance) or the most colloquial pronunciation (*gotta*, *didja*). On the whole, however, uniformity is the rule in our spelling.

The 18th century was different. There were conventions for spelling, but these conventions had no absolute binding force. Even in public documents produced by professional scribes one finds such variant forms as *speak*, *speake*, *speke*, and *speek* for the same word. In town records, ships' logs, and personal letters—the private and semipublic documents produced by those who were by no means professional writers—the amount of "originality" can be very great. This lack of uniformity in spelling is easily explained. Though learning was highly prized in colonial days, opportunities for education were not what we know today. As a consequence, the reading public was proportionately much smaller and the number, size, and frequency of newspapers a mere fraction of what we have now. Without widespread, uniform journalistic prose, any tendencies which existed toward individualistic spelling would be favored. Furthermore, there was essentially no established reference work to which a writer might go for information about the spelling of a word. Such a volume would come later, after independence, with the publication of the first American dictionary of the English language by Olmsted's contemporary, Noah Webster.[1] Webster, through the numerous editions of his *Dictionary* and the many spellers and other textbooks he wrote, is responsible more than anyone for the established norms of spelling which we today take for granted.

Gideon Olmsted was obviously not a professional writer, but neither was he illiterate. From the little we know of his boyhood in Hartford, Conn., it seems certain that before he went off to become the apprentice of some sea captain he had at least had the basic schooling in the three R's which Puritan families like his so highly esteemed.[2] The journal itself suggests that Olmsted was probably not unusual in writing abilities for a mariner of that time. The writing indicates a quill pen held firmly, with no shakiness, little blotting, no cramping of letters, and with even some embellishments. The spelling shows some knowledge of orthographic conventions, supplemented with a fairly shrewd ability to spell by ear when memory was not sufficient.

Scholars concerned with the history of American English naturally turn to whatever records of earlier times can be found in order to learn about the pronunciation of those times. They sift through the records of counties, townships, villages, and churches—the accounts of births, marriages, deaths, wills, sales of farms and houses, horses and implements—to find evidence about the speechways of our forebears.[3] Such evidence is combined with other information about the earlier history of a community— the record of its settlement, the parts of the British Isles (or elsewhere) from which the earliest settlers and the later immigrants came, the proportion, for example, of Devonshiremen to Ulster Scots; scholars attempt to find out from what other American settlements the townspeople might have come and to what areas their descendants might later have moved on; and, of course, they cannot neglect to assess the earlier documents in light of the pronunciation current in a community or an area at the present time.[4] But writings like Gideon Olmsted's journal are the prime source of information about English in colonial America.

To understand how the journal can be informative, we need to recognize a few facts about writing systems, about the changes which languages undergo over a period of time, and especially about the history of the English language. In an alphabetic writing system, such as we have, every letter should rightly represent one distinctive sound of the spoken language— always the same distinctive sound—and, the other way around, each sound should always be written with the same letter (or, extending a little, one sequence of letters like *ch* or *ee* might stand for a single sound and a single letter like *x* can represent a sequence of sounds). With such a regular system any person of normal intelligence can become literate in a relatively short time. After learning a system of equivalencies anyone should be able to write down correctly any new word he hears and to pronounce aloud correctly any new word he encounters in writing. This ideal situation always exists when a language community has just acquired an alphabetic system of writing. Some languages, like Finnish and Spanish, have approximately this kind of regularity after centuries of literacy. English, however, has not had an entirely consistent orthography since the Norman Conquest. There are several reasons for this unhappy situation (just as there have been several so far unsuccessful attempts to reform our spelling system). One problem is that the Latin alphabet has only five vowel letters (with *y* as a possible sixth) and English has many more vowel *sounds* to be represented, though using combinations like *ea, oa, ou, oi* helps to overcome the shortage.[5] Another cause of spelling irregularities is to be found in the pedantry of those who caused, for example, the insertion of an *o* into *people* because it comes ultimately from Latin *populus* and a *b* into *doubt* because the source of the word, again ultimately, is Latin *dubitum*—though Latin origin is really not relevant to day-by-day use of our language.

The main cause of irregularity in our spelling system, however, is language change. Any language changes over a period of time, in the words that it has and the meanings that it gives to these words, in the ways it puts words together to make sentences, and in the ways the words are pronounced. But even though the pronunciation of English has changed from century to century, English-speakers have been conservative—ultraconservative—about changing their ways of spelling. For example, the words *cat*, *car*, *calm*, and *call* once were spoken with the same vowel sound (made with the tongue low in the mouth and the mouth wide open) and so were naturally enough written with the same vowel letter. In the course of time the pronunciation of these and many similar words changed, the original vowel becoming three different vowel sounds according to what consonant followed it, so that now the vowel of *cat* is made with the tongue low in the front of the mouth, the vowel of *calm* and *car* with the tongue low in the center of the mouth (for most speakers), and the vowel of *call* with the tongue in a low back position. Common sense would dictate that where three different sounds are spoken three different letters should be written, but the Anglo-Saxon world has been extremely wary of changes in spelling, and we continue to write an *a* in all these words.

The split of one vowel into three vowels may be called sound divergence. The opposite, sound convergence, also occurs. The three words *mete*, *meet*, and *meat*, now homophonous, were originally all different in pronunciation. The first word was pronounced in two syllables because what we now call "silent *e*" was not silent until the 14th or 15th century. The word *meet* (and *green*, *keep*, *see*) had one vowel sound, the word *meat* (and *heap*, *clean*, *sea*, etc.) had another until the 18th century, when the two sounds fell together.

As a result of these (and other) phonic changes without parallel graphic changes, our spelling system is now less sound-oriented and more word-oriented. We cannot simply spell by ear but must learn the appropriate graphic form associated with a particular meaning. We cannot freely interchange *mete*, *meet*, and *meat*, nor *pear*, *pair*, and *pare*, though there would be little chance of misunderstanding if we did. In this respect we differ from the 18th century. Likewise, if each word has its appropriate spelling, it has only one spelling. In speaking many of us probably pronounce no *t* in *next day* though we do pronounce a *t* in *next evening*. Many of us "drop the *g*," at least occasionally, when we say *morning* and *evening*, *going* and *coming*, *something for nothing*, and the like. But it does not occur to us to write *next* sometimes and sometimes *nex*, nor to alternate, in writing, *mornin* with *morning*.[6] In this respect, too, we differ from the 18th century.

So far we have been discussing English as if it were a single unified and uniform language. On the contrary, it is and has always been diverse.

Tracing the history of the language is all the more challenging because of this diversity. In medieval England, as in other European countries at the time, dialect differences were considerable, reflecting the feudal society and the isolation of the era.[7] However, by the beginnings of what we call modern times—the age of Henry VIII and Elizabeth I—London was the firm center of a nation and not long thereafter the center of an empire. Not surprisingly, the speech of this area, southeastern England, became the basis of a national standard, the form of language used by all educated Englishmen, though less advantaged and less ambitious Englishmen still speak regional dialects, and Welshmen, Scotchmen, and Irishmen, educated or not, have no use for the so-called Received Pronunciation of the English upper and upper-middle classes.

The people who brought English to America came from all parts of the British Isles—Ireland, Scotland, Wales, and the various counties of England. These included the counties of southeastern England, to be sure (Gideon Olmsted's great-great-great-grandparents were from Essex),[8] but the sheer weight of proportions meant that the language of northern and western England would be most influential in shaping American English. This influence explains, in part at least, why American English is so different from the best known form of British English, the language of the queen and her family and most members of the "Establishment." American English has greater affinity with other dialects of England. Indeed, aside from vocabulary, there is little in American English that is exclusively American. Any feature of pronunciation or grammar in the English of the United States can usually also be found somewhere in Britain.

Another reason for the difference between Standard British English and the language of most Americans is that they have been developing separately, especially between the time the Americans became independent and the age of radio and the talking motion pictures, when the voices of more Britons began reaching the ears of more Americans and American voices likewise traveled to Britain. Standard British English has undergone certain sound changes which other dialects (American, Canadian, Irish, Scots, northern England) did not share in—at least, not directly. One of the most notable features of Standard British is that no *r* is pronounced in such words as *car, sure, hear, hard, short, morning*—that is, wherever *r* is final or followed by a consonant (but an *r* is pronounced in *very, narrow*, and the like, where a vowel sound follows). This loss of *r* in London speech may have started as early as the 16th century, if certain *r*-less spellings in documents of that time can be believed, but it did not catch on all at once. Apparently the *r*-less pronunciation was at first a usage of the lower classes, but during the 18th century—again apparently—it became established among the gentry.[9]

The founding of English colonies in America mostly took place during the 17th century, so it is not likely that the loss of *r* would have affected the language of the first generations of settlers. Later, however, before the rupture of political bonds between the united colonies and the mother country, the London dialect must have had an influence on at least some Americans simply because it was the standard, the prestige, form of English. Some Americans managed to travel to England or to send their sons there for study, British officers were sent out to the colonies by the king, and there was more commerce between London and the individual colonies than between one colony and another. This influence must have been felt primarily in the large ports—Boston, New York, Philadelphia, Baltimore, Charleston, and Savannah—and must have spread out, to greater or lesser extent, from them. In the United States today the *r*-less pronunciation is found in three general areas: eastern New England (of which Boston is the metropolis), New York City, and the South (excluding the Appalachians). The *r*-less pronunciation did not become established in the middle colonies (New Jersey, Pennsylvania, Delaware, Maryland) nor in western New England, where settlements began in the 17th century, before the emergence of this phonetic characteristic, and where, one would imagine, the influence of Britannia was less than in eastern New England.

Another sound change that took place in Standard British English at a slightly later time concerns the vowel sound we commonly call "short *a*." Most Americans pronounce the same vowel sound in *path* and *pass* as in *pat* and *pack;* this is the older state of affairs. At some time, and probably beginning in the 18th century, Standard British came to use a vowel made in the low central part of the mouth (like Ah!) when the following consonant is *f* (as in *half, craft*), *th* (*bath, rather*), *s* (*pass, last*), and sometimes before sequences like *mp* (*example*), *nd* (*demand, command*), and *ns* (*transfer, dance*) but before other consonants (*pat, pack*, etc.) it has the low front vowel sound that American English has in all these words. Many of the "broad *a*" pronunciations of Standard British have taken root in eastern New England, a sprinkling of them in New York and in eastern Virginia and the Carolinas; elsewhere in the United States they hardly exist.

In short, two pronunciation features, and probably others, could have spread in America but did not. One wonders if these pronunciations, or any one of them, once were more prevalent but declined in popularity with the withdrawal of British influence. Or is it the case that such phonic features were never more widespread than they are today? The city of Hartford is now in an area of *r*-pronunciations, but was it so when Gideon Olmsted grew up there? Did people then say *Ha'tfo'd* or *Hartford*, or did they possibly use both forms indifferently? Answers to questions such as these are, of course, hardly crucial in themselves, but a more thorough knowledge of the way our predecessors talked ought to be valuable in a general fashion, giving us a better understanding of them and of ourselves and of the ways in which human language changes.

We gain knowledge about the pronunciation of English in past times from various sources. One kind of source is the description given by people like Noah Webster, people who, with greater or lesser accuracy, told how speech sounds were made—but this sort of information is all too rare. Other scraps of evidence are supplied by rhymes and puns of earlier drama and narrative poetry.[10] Then, there are the surviving letters and records of bygone people, the famous and the humble, and perhaps more especially the humble, those who wrote more by ear than by the precepts of a spelling book. When we find in 18th-century writings such spellings as *woter* and *swollow*, we know that the original vowel sound of these words, made in the front part of the mouth, has been replaced, after *w*, by a vowel sound made in the back part of the mouth, which the writer felt was more properly indicated with an *o* than with an *a*. If we should find, in an older document, a spelling like *mornin* or *mornen* for *morning*, we would know that the writer pronounced an *n* sound rather than the *ng* sound at the end of this and similar words. Of course, the fact that *morning* appears in the document does not mean that the writer pronounced an *ng* there; it may only indicate that he or she knew what the conventional spelling was. Suppose, however, that we find *chicking* or *kitching* in contexts where we would expect *chicken* and *kitchen*, respectively. Such inverse spellings would indicate that the writer was in the habit of putting on paper the letters *ng* whenever the sound of *n* (in his or her pronunciation) came at the end of a word—in other words, that the writer rhymed *chicken* and *picking*. Gideon Olmsted's "Journal of an Intended Voyage From New London to Guadeloupe in the Sloop *Seaflower*" is just such a document. For one who has some knowledge of the history of English, of the kind partially sketched in these pages, Olmsted's writing tells something about his pronunciation. We can, to some degree, figure out how he must have spoken. But still some mysteries remain.

The journal is not long. It contains fewer than 6,000 running words (that is, the count of every occurrence of every word used). When a list of the different words is made, like the glossary that follows, the total is seen to be about a thousand. The words most repeated are the little items like *the*, *of*, *for*, *was* ("wors"), and *and*, the hardest workers in any stretch of English speech or writing. Then there are words like *ship*, *sail*, *hatches*, and *quarterdeck* which recur because of the nature of this particular story. Altogether, then, while there is not a large vocabulary here, many of the words appear more than once, and in many instances a word is written in two or three ways.

This variation in spelling provides a handy place to begin our investigation of Olmsted's language. Why didn't the author spell words the same way each time? There seem to be five different reasons for variation:

1. Gideon, like all of us, sometimes makes a slip of the pen (*bfore = before*).

2. In a few instances where a proper name is involved he seems not to be sure of it (*Horſton = Hurſson = Houſon = Horſtton*).

3. For some words he knows the conventional spelling and sometimes writes it, or attempts to write it, but at other times he puts down something which is more appropriate to his pronunciation (*ol = all*).

4. For some words he knows varying pronunciations and so indicates now one, now the other (*consarned = consurned*).

5. All other variant spellings are just graphic equivalents for the author, equally valid ways of indicating a word (*fleat= fleet*).

There can be little doubt that all five of these reasons are responsible for Captain Olmsted's variable orthography, but there are also problems in classifying: in some instances it is difficult or impossible to say whether different spellings represent different pronunciations or are only different ways of representing the same thing. Let's examine the variations in greater detail.

Slips of the pen. Consider these pairs:

Adrolmaty/admorlty
asinſtance/aſsiſtance
bfore/before
Box/Fox
Iinglish/Inglish

In each pair the second word would seem to be the intended one, whereas the first is simply the result of the fact that the writer was a human being. *Adrolmoty* has letters in the wrong order; *asinſtance* shows over-anticipation, the premature insertion of a letter which comes later; in *bfore* he has omitted a letter; in *Box* the author has put down the wrong letter; in *Iinglish* he has inserted an extra one (but note that *I* more correctly denotes our pronunciation of the word than the *E* which we use).

If the errors in the above words are obvious enough, it is not hard to spot the mistakes in the following words and to figure out what the author intended, even though in these instances the word appears only once. Like the words above, the words below exhibit errors due to omission of letters, insertion of extra letters, or transpositions. In parentheses we suggest what was probably intended.

amedoilyty   (amediotly, i.e., *immediately*)
bter   (beter, better)
Dexteryti   (Dexterity)
Diffolkety   (Diffokelty, Diffekolty)
deſorbance   (deſtorbance)

integlenence	(intelegence)
lyvee	(lyve)
Nickeſale	(Nickelaſe, i.e., *Nicholas*)

Cases of uncertainty. Our hero seems to have had trouble at times in grasping certain names which perhaps he heard only a few times. We have already mentioned, above, the various spellings that appear in the journal for the name *Houston.* He also has variant ways of indicating the names *Honduras, Leogane, Ramsdell,* and *Ross,* as the reader may see by consulting the glossary, and these variations seem to suggest confusion, rather than scribal error or use of equivalent ways of representing the same sounds.

Once we have identified the slips of the pen and the instances of the author's uncertainty, we are better able to assess what pronunciations he meant to indicate by his spellings in the remainder of the material.

Conventional spelling vs. ear spelling. There are instances where the author has undoubtedly been influenced by his memory (sometimes imperfect) of spelling conventions and, finding the conventions in conflict with what his ear tells him, vacillates between the message of his ear and the message of his mind's eye. It is obvious that Olmsted had some knowledge of conventional spelling: he consistently writes *people* just that way, though no speaker of English has ever pronounced anything that the *o* might stand for; similarly, he always has *l* in *could* (or *cold* or *kold*), though no such consonant has ever been pronounced in that word; [11] he writes *Ph* at the beginning of *Philadelphia,* where an ear-speller might well have used *F.* It is equally obvious, of course, that he was not guided by convention alone.

The conflicts between convention and the author's ears can be discussed with reference to several groups of words. In two groups we find alternation between the letters *a* and *o*:

    ol/all
    olmost/all morſt
    bole/boal [ball]

but in other words we find only *o* where convention requires *a*, with one exception:

whot	worf	colled
wotch	worter	*but*
wor	quorter	Salt
wonted	squolle	

As we have seen a vowel sound once made in the low front part of the mouth (and represented by the letter *a*) came to be replaced by a vowel sound made in the low back part of the mouth. This happened when the vowel in question was preceded by the sound of *w* (including *quarter* and *squally,* of course) and when followed by an *l.* Conventional spelling still uses the letter *a* in such words, but Olmsted, when guided by his ear, prefers *o*. We should note here that Gideon uses the letter-group *au* only once, in *August*, and he never uses *aw*. Instead he uses *oe* (*joes, loes* = *jaws, laws*), *ow* (*drow, sow* = *draw, saw*), or just *o* (*brote, fote* = *brought, fought*). Note also the compromise *oa* used once for *ball* and once for the last syllable of *tomahawk*.

Here is another group of words in which we may suspect a conflict between convention and what the writer usually said:

jeʃ/Jest	fiʃ
cep/cept	a crost
pleason/pleasont	hole
preson/preaʃont	mold
Seckont/seckond	Arnnorl
tol/told	
cowl/cold	

Quite likely when words ended in a cluster of consonants like *st, pt, nd, ld,* our author was inclined to simplify the pronunciation by omitting the last consonant. Quite naturally he would simplify the spelling likewise. We find spellings of this sort in numerous documents of the 17th and 18th centuries,[12] and anybody with good ears can hear today the pronunciation of *cold* and *around*, for instance, without a *d*. We notice that Olmsted, while omitting the *t* of *fist*, adds the same letter to *across;* he writes *cold* with and without a *d*, leaves out the *d* of *Arnold* and *hold* ("Wee stove two hogsheds of Molaʃses in the fore hole . . ."), and adds a *d* to *mole* (a breakwater built to protect a harbor, or a harbor so protected). *Mold* instead of *mole* and *hole* instead of *hold*, and the writing of both *tol* and *told* for the same word suggest that no *d* was pronounced in any of these words.

We find other examples of inverse spellings in the next group of words:

mornind/morning
nockind/Nocking/knocking
villing/villin
Demming/Demmin
a Crucind, yoʃeind [using]
a rowing, a standing, a thinking

It seems probable that Olmsted said, at least part of the time, *mornin, standin, thinkin,* with a final *n* rather than *ng*. He was aware, however, that convention required a written consonant letter after the *n*, and sometimes he got the right one down. He mistakenly thought that *villain* should also be written with a consonant after the *n*. Of course, his *knocking* shows knowledge of convention, and his *nocking* indicates that his concern was not deep. When he writes *know* for *no*, we see convention winning out, though in the wrong place.

Alternative pronunciations. Next we consider the possibility that when Captain Olmsted wrote a word in more than one way it was because he was familiar with more than one pronunciation. In the preceding section we noted his familiarity with spelling conventions. We must also note his ability to figure out a fairly accurate way of representing words as he pronounced them and heard them pronounced. Such forms as *menchon, ither, hith, kivred* he certainly did not learn from a speller, but they tell us more about how he spoke than the "correct" *mention, either, height,* and *covered* would do.

We are probably observing the written forms of alternative pronunciations in these three pairs:

git/get
rebbels/rubbels
consarned/consurned

Git in place of *get* was recorded as early as 1648,[13] and *rubbel* would seem to be a not unlikely variant of *rebel*. The last pair requires a little more explanation. In the 15th century the vowel *e* changed to *a* when it preceded *r*; *ferre, hert, sterve* became *far, heart, starve,* and for *sergeant* we still have the old spelling but the new pronunciation. This change took place irregularly, however, so that some words changed pronunciation in some dialects but not in others. Thus, where standard English has *serve, certain, learn,* and *early,* one can even today encounter in rural areas such pronunciations as *sarve, sartain, larn,* and *arly,* and these must have been more frequent in past times. Gideon Olmsted writes *clark* (still the standard British pronunciation of *clerk*), *sartenly, sarvis,* and *starn,* but in a more bookish word, *determined,* he writes *e*.[14]

Another set of words requiring comment is this:

pinted/pointed
hyst, jind, quilling
boyl, boys

In the speech of some people some words with *oy* came to be pronounced instead with "long *i*"; thus *point* and *pint* became identical, *poison* was pronounced *pizen,* and *join* occurs in poems of the time rhyming with *fine.* Various records have such spellings as *implyment* for *employment, pint* for *point,* and, inversely, *loyable* for *liable.* After a *k* or *g* sound this original *oy* developed—in the speech of some people—into something like *wi,* and that is why Olmsted writes *quiling* where we would put *coiling.* A grammar published in 1797 reprehends the pronunciation of *coil* and *coin* as *quile* and *quine,* but the corresponding pronunciation of *choir* is the only pronunciation we have today. The pronunciation of *going* as *gwine,* which perhaps because of the minstrel show tradition we associate with southern blacks, shows up in records of colonial New England and still exists in local dialects in the mother country itself.[15] Then, we should note that where Olmsted writes *boyl* (referring to the sore on Hezekiah Burnham's foot) he may very likely have said *bile,* which, in this meaning, comes from Old English *byle* and which, before the 17th century, was pronounced differently from the verb we associate with teakettles, from Old French *boillir.* The word *boys*, however, was probably pronounced in just the way we pronounce it.

Consider this last set of words:

    frinds, Ginnorel, innomy
    Contenentol, contented, Gentleman, attemp
    lenght, strenght

We have no variation in the writing of the same word, but rather two different spellings (and pronunciations) for the same original vowel, an *e* before a nasal consonant (*m, n, ng*). Such pronunciations as *pinny* and *gineral* are still common in some areas of our country, and research shows that they were common also in earlier times.[16] It is interesting to note, though impossible to explain, that Olmsted has *i* in a few of these words and *e* in others. (Why he writes *lenght* and *strenght* is a riddle. If he had written *height* and *weight*, one might explain the first pair as being formed in part by analogy with the latter pair. Olmsted wrote, in fact, *hith* and *wait*.)

Graphic equivalents. In nearly all other instances in which we find one word written two or more ways, we may assume that these were equivalent ways, to Olmsted and his contemporaries, of indicating the same word. Such equivalencies help us to interpret the spellings used for other words. For example, Captain Gideon writes *kuck, luck,* and *tuck* where we would write *cook, look,* and *took*. Did the three words sound different in his time from the way they are pronounced now? We might think so, but when we recognize that *foot* is also written *fut* in the journal, we are inclined to conclude that, rather than a difference of sound, we are here dealing with a wider use of the letter *u*, as compared with the spelling practices of our own times. Similarly, when we find *short* where we would write *shirt*, we might think that the *o* suggests a different pronunciation from our own. But when we see the word *hurt* written that way (with *u*) and also *hort*, we can conclude that the two words rhymed then, as they do now.

There are several kinds of graphic differences which we know at once have nothing to do with differences of pronunciation. Words are spelled with capital letters or small letters (*sword/Sword, a Clok/a clock*) for what seems to us to be pure whimsy, but certainly nothing that has to do with pronunciation. The way space is used, we can be sure, indicates nothing of a phonic nature; we find *a long* and *along, any thing* alongside *anything*, and we accept these as equivalent so far as pronunciation goes. We see the long form of *s* interchanging with the shorter version (*a Croʃt/a crost, Molaʃses/molasses,* etc.), but do not expect these to suggest different pronunciations. Even the doubling of consonant letters, which in our present scheme denotes something about the difference in the way the preceding vowel letter should be interpreted (compare *diner* and *dinner*, for instance), seems to be less functional in the journal; we find *swivvels* and *swivels, libborty* and *liborty,* etc, but no pair of words which suggest different pronunciations because the consonant letter is doubled in one word and not in the other.

A "silent *e*" is used, as now, to indicate that the preceding vowel is the "long" one. Thus we find *did* and *dide* (= died), *rum* and *rume* (= room). But such alternate spellings as *haveing* and *having*, *oute* and *out*, *fleate* and *fleet* tell us that the *e* is often more decorative than functional.

Elsewhere we find equivalent graphs somewhat similar to the usage of our times. The sound of *k* is indicated by *c*, *k*, and *ck* (*a Clok* = a clock, *amara-kan* = amarecon, *cold* = kold). The sound of *j* is represented by *j*, *g*, and *dg* (*Gentleman* vs. *Jentolmen*, *Judg* = *Jug*, *Bridg* = *Bridge*). The letter *c* is not used much for the sound of *s* (note *sitte* for *city*), but it turns up, oddly enough, in *Pencolvany*. The name *Hezekiah* contains the only instance of the letter *z*.[17] Elsewhere we find the sound of *z* indicated by *s*, *ss*, and *c* (*breas*, *pryse*, *crucers*/*crusers*, *mussel*, *dusſon*, *soundance*).

Ways of spelling vowel sounds are more numerous in the journal, as they still are. *Ee* and *ea* and even *eea* are equivalent (*keep*/*keap*/*keeap*, *fleet*/*fleat*, *agreed*/*agread*). *Ea* also interchanges with "long *a*" (*papers*/*peapers*, *take*/*teake*, *pare*/*pear*), which can also be represented by *ai* (*made*/*maid*, *mate*/*mait*, *plaſe*/*plais*), *Ou* and *ow*, not surprisingly, are equivalent (*down*/*down*, *owr*/*our*, *trowſes*/*trouſes*). *I* and *y* interchange in stressed position (*friday*/*fryday*, *miles*/*myles*, *nite*/*nyte*/*night*, *kil*/*kyl*); for final unstressed *y* the letter *e* is sometimes used (*mortely*/*mortolle*, *slitle*/*slitely*/*Slytole*).

Written records are not tape recordings, of course. We cannot tell from the spellings just how close to our vowel sounds were the sounds that Gideon Olmsted and his contemporaries made. We can only observe that he had the same vowel sound in *keep*, *fleet*, and *agree*, just as we do; the same sound in *place*, *take*, and *paper*, and so forth. Only occasionally do we suspect differences. Where we make a "short *e*" sound in *heavy*, *pleasure*, *ready*, and *says*, Olmsted may have had a "long *a*" (*havy*, *plaſure*, *rayde*, *sase*); perhaps the same is true of *whether* (*whether*/*whather*/*wheather*). And where we pronounce *ch* in *fortune*, *furniture*, and *venture*, we may be fairly sure that Gideon Olmsted, like Noah Webster, had a *t* sound (*forten*, *fornetur*, *ventor*).[18]

The most vexing problem remains. Why does our author insert the letter *r* into so many words (*sharnt*, *worter*, *meadorſsons*)? Why is there the variation between *smol* and *smorl*, *thot*(*e*) and *thort*(*e*), *histed* and *hirsted*, and other such pairs? Did he pronounce an *r* in *shan't* and *water*, occasionally pronounce one in *small* and *thought* but not always?

We can make certain observations. For one, the words which appear in two or more variant forms, one with an *r* and one without, are almost all words which historically had no *r*:

Comma(r)nder	pi(r)sto(r)l
hi(r)sted	smo(r)l
mu(r)st	tho(r)t(e)
wo(r)nted	all morst/olmost

The one exception is the word *fo(r)ther*. A second observation is that among words appearing only once each in the journal, some are written with an *r* which historically does not belong there. For example, *tavern*, which Gideon writes *tarvern*, comes from Middle English *taverne*, which comes from Old French *taverne*, which in turn comes from Latin *taberna*. It never had an *r* in its first syllable. The following are other words from the journal with nonhistoric *r*'s:

arft	larst	raʃkeorl
Corffen	lorst	sharnt
farʃt	marʃter	torte [taut]
horʃspittol	meadorʃsons	wors [was]
Josior [Josiah]	Orʃtreg [Ostrich]	worter
jurnnorl	prʃiʃhon	

We note that in the word for *position* the *r* seems to act as a kind of vowel. In all other cases of "inserted" *r* the insertion appears after a vowel—at the end of the word in *Josiah*, before a consonant in all the other words—but never before a vowel. Examining other words in the glossary, we note that with two exceptions there are no words with an historic *r* (such as *corn* and *harbor*) from which the *r* is missing. The two exceptions are *a thote* (= athwart), a seaman's term, and *paʃsol*, a New England colloquialism derived from *parcel*.

It seems probable, then, but not certain, that no *r* was pronounced after a vowel in Gideon Olmsted's speech, a linguistic feature which, as we have seen, had become or was becoming the accepted thing in Standard British English. To say that the *r* had disappeared would not be entirely accurate, for with its loss the preceding vowel became lengthened or drawled out. This was especially true of the low front or low center vowel of *hard, large, March*, etc. and the low back vowel of *horn, north, storm*, etc. The same lengthening of the same or similar vowel sounds was taking place before certain consonants, such as *f*, *v*, and *s* (*aft, coffin, tavern, last, ostrich*) and after *w* (*want, was, water*) where an earlier *a* had become, as we have seen, the back vowel which Olmsted preferred to represent with the letter *o*. Thus it must have seemed natural to use *ar* and *or* in these and similar words to indicate the prolonged vowels that were pronounced in them. And when *r* was lost in unstressed syllables, as in *color, eastward, liberty*, the slurred vowel sound that results is about identical with the vowel sound in the second syllable of *rascal* and *medicine* and the first syllable of *position*. If one has learned to write an *r* in *color, eastward, liberty*, etc., what could be more natural than to introduce an *r* in the writing of *rascal, medicine, position,* and the like?

The foregoing is theory, not a factual account, for the facts are not known. There are possible arguments against the theory. One such argument is that Hartford and the Connecticut River valley is now an area in which *r*'s are pronounced. However, it is not hard to believe that this linguistic feature was once more widespread than now and then declined with the decline of British prestige. Another problem is that there is a group of words in which *r* might have been written but was not. Why, for instance, does the journal have *arft* but *after, Corſſen* but *Coffe*? Why is there no *r* in *glasſ*? Against these unanswerable questions we can simply note that orthographic consistency is obviously not Gideon's greatest virtue. The most troubling question is this: if the author did not pronounce an *r* in *arms, before, harbor, New York, Saturday,* and about 150 other words which appear in the journal, how is it that he never fails to write it in these words?[19]

To conclude as we began, we may say that the fascinating story Gideon Olmsted tells is relayed in language that has its own fascination. We see the author as an individualist in his manner of writing, but also as a child of his times. The journal, in conjunction with other records, helps us to understand better the history of our language, which should aid us in a better understanding of ourselves.

NOTES

[1] For a survey of Webster's accomplishments see Harry R. Warfel, *Noah Webster, Schoolmaster to America* (New York: Octagon, 1936), and Joseph H. Friend, *The Development of American Lexicography, 1798–1864* (Paris: Mouton, 1967).

[2] Louis F. Middlebrook, *Captain Gideon Olmsted, Connecticut Privateersman, Revolutionary War* (Salem, Mass.: Newcomb & Gauss Co., 1933), p. 2.

[3] Evidence of this sort, assembled by scores of earlier investigators, is the raw material of George Philip Krapp's monumental work, *The English Language in America*, 2 vol. (New York: The Century Co., for the Modern Language Assoc. of America, 1925). It is, of course, impossible to deal with American English in isolation. For the longer history of British English we have not only the evidence of literary and nonliterary documents but also, from the 16th century on, the testimony of orthoepists who, for one reason or another, described their own form of English. These descriptions—and their interpretation—are studied by E. J. Dobson, *English Pronunciation 1500–1700*, 2 vol. (Oxford: Clarendon Press, 1968).

[4] The scientific study of speech differences from one community to another is called dialect geography or linguistic geography. Beginning in 1928 a group of researchers, under the direction of Hans Kurath, undertook the careful investigation of regional differences in language use throughout New England—an investigation later extended by other scholars to other parts of the United States and still in progress. The results of the original research project have been published as *The Linguistic Atlas of New England* (Providence, R.I.: Brown University, 1939–43), edited by Kurath. Various specialized studies have made use of these data and others collected subsequently, most notably *The Pronunciation of English in the At-*

lantic States (Ann Arbor: University of Michigan Press, 1961), by Kurath and Raven I. McDavid, Jr.

[5] The number of vowel *sounds* in English is about 14, with some dialects having more, some fewer. Nearly every speaker of English will recognize that the words in each group below have the same vowel sound regardless of the spelling and each group has a different vowel sound from any of the other groups:

hut, young, blood	two, truth, troop
we, weed, weave	took, put
wit, myth	toe, dough, soap
way, wait, wake	law, ought, cause,
wed, bread, said	spa, not
sad, plaid	toy, moist
sigh, side, type	brown, cloud

Any of our unabridged dictionaries will provide, in its prefatory sections, information about the way each of these vowel-units is pronounced, i.e., whether the tongue is higher or lower, more forward or more back, and whether the lips are more rounded or more stretched during the articulation of the vowel sound.

[6] Although it is usual to speak of "dropping the *g*" when one says *mornin* and *coughin* (identical with *coffin*) instead of *morning* and *coughing*, in reality this is the replacement of one nasal sound ('ng'), made with the back of the tongue up, by another nasal sound ('n') made with the tip of the tongue up. Notice also that this exchange only happens in the unaccented syllable *ing*. Nobody ever "drops the *g*" in *sing, hang, young,* or *long,* for example.

[7] Scholars divide the history of the English language into three periods, Old, Middle, and Modern English. Old English (or Anglo-Saxon) is the period before the Norman Conquest (1066); Middle English is the language from the Conquest to 1500; and Modern English is the language since that date.

[8] Middlebrook, *Olmsted,* p. viii.

[9] Krapp, *English Language,* vol. 2, pp. 217–31, has a careful survey of words spelled without *r* in which, historically, an *r* belongs and of words in which a nonhistoric *r* has been inserted by semiskilled writers.

[10] An example of an informative rhyme is this bit of nursery doggerel:

Old Mother Goose, when she wanted to wander,
Would fly through the air on a very fine gander.

Wander and *gander* do not rhyme for us, but this nursery rhyme suggests that they once did, and similarly other sources attest to the fact that *want* and *grant* once rhymed, as did *water* and *scatter.* The inescapable conclusion is that the letter *a* once represented the same sound after *w* as it did after other consonants and that the sound has changed in this position over a period of time—but the way of writing it has not changed.

An example of a pun which is informative comes from a comparatively recent work, Lewis Carroll's *Alice in Wonderland* (1865). The Mock Turtle, reminiscing about his childhood school in the sea, remarks that he and his fellow students called their turtle schoolmaster "Tortoise."

"Why did you call him Tortoise, if he wasn't one?" Alice asked.
"We called him Tortoise because he taught us," said the Mock Turtle angrily, "really you are very dull!"

Many of us may also feel dull about this until we realize that Carroll and his Victorian readers did not pronounce an *r* in *tortoise,* so that the word was homophonous with *taught us.*

[11] *Could* is from old English *cūthe,* Middle English *coude.* The spelling with *l* arose by analogy with *would* and *should.*

[12] Krapp, *English Language,* vol. 2, pp. 25–28.

[13] Krapp, *English Language,* vol. 2, p. 98.

[14] But a spelling *detarmen* appears frequently for this word in the town records of Groton, Mass., from 1664 on. See Krapp, *English Language*, vol. 2, p. 170.

[15] Krapp, *English Language*, vol. 2, pp. 199–200.

[16] Krapp (*English Language*, vol. 2, pp. 96–98) cities from various sources *ind, inemy, sintence, ginrous, frind, aginst, primises*, among others, for *end, enemy, sentence, generous, friend, against, premises*.

[17] Quite similarly, the surviving account book of a blacksmith named John Bate, dating from the 1770's, uses the letter *z* only in spelling the names *ezre* (Ezra), *ezrel* (Israel), *abanazor* (Ebenezer), and *zakel* (Ezekiel). See Harold Whitehall, "The Orthography of John Bate of Sharon, Connecticut (1700–1784)," *American Speech* 22, no. 1, pt. 2 (1947).

[18] Indeed, Webster was quite adamant in his insistence that *creature, nature, virtue*, and the like should be pronounced *creater, nater, virtoo*. Such insistence, of course, indicates that he knew of another pronunciation or other pronunciations. In his *Elementary Spelling Book* of 1843, Webster, near the end of his life, declared that *natshur* and *jointshur*, though common pronunciations in England and America for *nature* and *jointure*, were not "the most elegant." He did, however, concede that "*nateyour, jointyour*" were acceptable pronunciations. See Friend, *American Lexography*, pp. 73–74.

[19] H. Rex Wilson has studied the orthography used in the journal of one Abijah Willard, born 1724 in Lancaster, Mass. Willard, like Olmsted, frequently inserted a written *r* where one would assume no *r* was pronounced; unlike Olmsted, however, he often omits *r* (for example, in the words we write *are, boarded, marched, number, party*) where it historically belongs. Thus Willard's writing suggests in two ways that *r* had ceased to be pronounced after vowels in his speech: he omits the letter *r* where it might be expected, and he inserts an unexpected letter *r*. Olmsted does only the latter. See H. Rex Wilson, "From Postulates to Procedures in the Interpretation of Spellings," Lawrence M. Davis, ed., *Studies in Linguistics in Honor of Raven I. McDavid, Jr.* (University, Ala.: University of Alabama Press, 1972), pp. 215–28.

GLOSSARY

Charles W. Kreidler

THE ALPHABETICAL LIST which follows contains essentially all the vocabulary used by Gideon Olmsted in his journal, exactly as he wrote the words, including proper names and abbreviations. All the variant spellings—but not variant capitalization—for each word are listed, with the one less familiar usually given first. Inflected forms, like plurals of nouns, past tense of verbs, and other common derivatives are listed, indented, after the basic form. Irregular inflected forms also appear separately in the alphabetical listing. Thus the entry for the verb *take* looks like this:

> teake/take
>   taking
>   teaken/teakon
>   tuck

and the past tense form *tuck* is also listed separately. In the few instances where a word or the form of a word seems to be something that our journalist clearly did not intend to write, the item is enclosed in parentheses.
Finally, it must be noted that the present-day equivalent of the words glossed here is given—in brackets—only in cases where confusion might arise.

a
Able
ablige
  a bliged
a bout/about
above
a burd/a bor/a bord/a board
a Clok/a clock
a comming
a cordingly
a crost/a Croſt
a Crucind   [acruising]
action
the Active
Admorel
admorlty/(Adrolmoty)
advyse
after

a fut
a fyting
a gain/again
aggony
a going
agread/agreed
a hed
all/ol
  at tol
all morſt/olmost
a long/along
a long syde/a long side
a low/alow
  aloud/a loued/aloued
Amaraka
amarakan/amerecan/amarecon/Amarecan
  amarekans
(amedoilyty)   [immediately]

120

A Mr/at Mr   [A.M.]
a mung
an
and
a nother/another
a nuf
any
any thing/anything
apeailed
April
are   [air]
are
arft/aft
arm
  arms
Arnnorl, Mager Ginnorel
a rowing
as
a Shore
a sleeap
aſſiſtence/(asinſtance)
ask
  asked
a standing
a Starn
a state/a State/astate
at
a thinking
a thote   [athwart]
attemp
  atemps
  attempted
August
a way/away
Axſes
Back
bad
bag
Bar   [bear]
  Baring
barel
  barels
bay
Bearry, Capt
bee/be
  being
beeaf
before/(bfore)
beged
begun
Behavure
behind
beleaved

beloe
belong
  Belonging
  belonged
best
betwixt
bin
bits
blud
  bluddy
blunderbuſh
  blunderbuſhes
the Boge
bole   [bowl]
bole/boal   [ball]
  bols
boome
bord
  borded
bore
bote
  botes
both
bound
bowsprit
boyl
Boys
brave
breas
Breath   [breathe]
Brig/(bring)
bring
  bringing
  brote
British/brittish
brod side/brodeside/brode Side
  brodesides
broke
brote
(bter)
Buckland, John
bulk hed
bullit
Bured
burn
  Burnning
  burnt
Burnham, Hezekiah
But/but
by
cabben/Cabbin
Cabol/Cable
came

cannon
cape
  capes
Capt/Capten/Cap
  Captens
care
cargo
carredg
Cartorges
cary
  cared/cayred/Caryed/Carid
case
cep/cept   [kept]
chance
chear
  chears
Checked
Chest
Cheſtor
choes
Clark
Clark, David
clearred
cloes
Coffe
cold/could/kold
  coldnot/koldnot
colled
Com/come/cum
  came
Comiſsion/Commisſion
Commarnd
Committe
Comnr/Commarnder/Commander/
    Commandor/Commarndor
comp/compony/Company
compannun way
condemn
condiſhon
Confyning/Confyneing
  confynd
Congris/Congress
consarned/consurned
Contented
Contonentol
the Convenſion/Convention
Convoy
cord
Corel, William
Corffen
Corn
Corps
Cort
Couhorns

cowld/cowl
crafts
Credet
Cros
Croſe, Robert
Crowbar
Crucer
  Crucers/crusers
  (a Crucind)
Crufe
cryed
cullors/culors
cuntremen/Cuntramen
cut
Dam/D
  Damd
dare
Day
  Days
Daylyte/Daylite
deal
deceaved
December
deck
ded
Defend
Dellowware river
Demmin, Isrel/Demming
Desine
deſired
deſtorbance
deſtreſs
determened
deth
(Dexteryti)
Did
  didnot
Dide/Dyde   [died]
(Diffolkety)
Disscurridg
Doctor
doe/Doe
  dont
  Did
  done
dollars
doun/Doun
dranck
dreſsed
drove
drow
  drowing
  dru
dry

duks   [ducks]
duſson
Dutchmans
Duty
dye   [die]
  dide/dyde
E
  Easttorn
  Eastword
easy
  easaly
Edmonſon, Capt
Egharbor
els
end
enter
ever
every
  everyone
  every thing
exſchanged
exſept/exept
exſpected
far
farſt
fasned
fathom
feat [feet]
fel
felings
fellow
fiſ   [fist]
fixing
fleat/fleate/fleet
flesh
flog
flowr   [floor]
for
fore
fore   [four]
foresail
fornetur
forrod/forword
fors
forten
forther/fother   [further]
fote
foul
  fouls
found
Fox, Isrel
franſway, cape/(fran)
French

frenchman
frenchmen
frinds
from
fryday/friday
fue
ful
Furbs, Eliflet/Forbs
furst
fut/foot
  feat
fyer flaſkes
fynd
  found
fyre/fyer
  fyreing/fyring
  fyred/fired
fyte
  fote
gail   [jail]
gale
gallons
gallont
Gaudeloope
gave
Gentleman
  Jentolmen
Ginnorl/Ginnorel
git/get
  got
give
  giving
  gave
glad
glaſ
  glaſses
Glaſssco
glory
gloves
God
goe/go
  went
Gonnale, Mr Antony
good
goods
Gorden
got
gotes   [goats]
grannades
Granteer   [Grand Terre]
Grappled
grate   [great]
grog

ground
gun
  guns
haches/hatches
hatch way
had
  hadnot
half
halled/hailled
Hambottom, Mr
hand
  hands
handdercheaf
harber
  harbers
harde/hard
hart
hat
hath
have
  haveing/having
  had
havy
he
  his
  him
heard
hed
  heds
Helm
Helth
Hibs, Lut
hiſt
  histed/hirſted
hit
hobblen   [hobbling]
  hobbled
Hodg, John
hogsheds
hol/hole   [haul]
  holled
hole   [hole]
hole   [whole]
hole   [hold]
home
  homeword
Homes, Mr
hopeed
hor   [her]
  hors
horn
horſspittol
Horſton/Hurſson/Hurſton/

Houſon/Horſtton, Thommos
hot
hour
  hours
hous/house
hove
how
hulks
Hundoros/hondorſ/
    hordoron/hondoras, Bay of
hurt/hort
hye
I
  me/(my)
  my
  myne
if
in
inbargo
including
incurriging
informd
Ingagd
  ingagement
Inglish/(Ingliſh)
  inglishman
innomy
inpoſseble
inſtant
Instorement   [instrument]
(integlenence)   [intelligence]
intend
  intended
into
Invyted
Irons
Island
it
ither
Jackson, Mr
Jemeco/Jameco
Jentolmen
Jenuary
Jest/just
Jibed
Jind
Joes   [jaws]
Joes
Johnson, Mr
Joſior, Capt
Judg/Judge
July
Jumped

June
Jurnnorl/jurnorl
Juſtis
keeap/keep/keap
  cep/cept
kil/kyl
  killed
kind
Kingstoun
kivred   [covered]
Know   [no]
Knu
kold/cold/could
  koldnot/coldnot
  koopes
  kuck   [cook]
  kucked
Ladder
lame
  lameſness
land
  Landed
larbord
large
larst/larſte
  larſted
lately
Latt/Ltt   [latitude]
lay
  layd
leags
leake
Leave
  leaving
  left
leg
  legs
lemented
lend
lenght
let
libborty/libberty
little
loded
Loes   [laws]
long
Longisland
lorſt
lose   [lose]
  loſd   [loosed]
Loſtafs
louſse   [lousy]
luck   [look]

luked
luckely
Lugan/Lu Jan
lunnon/London
Lut/Lutnnont/Lutennont
  Leutennont
Lybild
lye
  lay
lyfe
(lyvee)   [live]
made/maid/mad
main
mait/mate
  mates
man
  men
  maned/manned
man of wor
men of wor
many
March
marſter
Marted, Aaron
matter
me
meadorſsons
mean while
menchon
ment
meſtruſt
mettol
mis
miſsorry
Molaſses/molasses
mold
moment
  moments
monday
Montego
mony
more
mornind/morning/mornning
morst   [most]
mortolle/mortolly
motion
mouth
movement
Mr
much
mud
murſ/murſt/must
Muskit

mussel   [muzzle]
mutton
my
  myne
  my self/myself
(my)   [me]
myles/miles
myte
nayms/Names
Negro
  Negroes
never
next
(Nickeʃale), Cape
the Nigers
Nine
nockind/Nocking/knocking
Non/none
Nor
North
  N
  Nward
  NW
not
nothing
Notwithstanding
nue   [knew]
Nulondon
number
Numoros
Nuyork/Nue york/Nueyork/NueYork/
    Nueyorke
Ny/Nye
  Nyor
Nyte/nite/Night
  Nytes
O
ocasiond
october
ods
of
of   [off]
offeʃsor
  offeʃsers
offred
ol/all
old
olmost/all morʃt
Olmʃted, Gideon
on
onbent
once
one/(ond)

onlaid
onned
ontye
onweg
  onweged
open
or
Oray, Mr. John
order
  orders
  ordred
the Orʃtreg   [Ostrich]
other
out/oute
over
Owr/our
  owre selves/owr Selves
part
  parted
party
paʃseg/passedg
paʃsol
paʃsonger
  passengers
pay
  payd
payn
peaceble
peaper/paper
  peapors/peapers/papers
pear/pare   [pair]
Pencolvany
people
phaledelfa/phaledefpha/Pholedelfa
pinted/poynted
pirʃtol/piʃtol
  piʃtorls
plaid/played
plank
plaʃe/Plais/place
plaʃure
pleaʃed
pleason/pleasont
pled
P Mr   [P.M.]
poore
port
Port a Prince/Portteprince/Pt prince
Port Morant
pouder
  pounders
power
preaʃont/preson

pressed
peiʃnor
priʃnors/priʃners
priʃiʃhon
proffit
Proʃhon/Proʃhone, Mr
proveal   [prevail]
proved
provishons/provissions
pryse/prise/Pryes
prysemarster
pryvit
Pryvitteer
pul
pumped
put
Pyrots
pytty
queek
queort   [quiet]
quiling   [coiling]
   quilled
quorter
   quorters
quorterdeck/quortardeck/quorter deck
quortermaʃter/quortermarʃter
Raked
Ramsdol/Ramsdorl/Ramdorl, Aq-
   willor/Aquilla
ran
raʃkeorl
rayde
Readeisland/red Island
Reaʃon/reason
rebble/Rebbel
   Rebbels/rubbels
refueʃed
resistance
reʃt/Rest
returnned
rigging
Ringbolt
Robbords/Robberts, George
Robson/Robborson, Robbort/Robbert
rode
(Rodeʃilland)
Rows, George/Roʃs
the Royal george
ruddor/rudder
rum
rume   [room]
Run
   running

ran
ryte
Safe
said
saim
Sale/Sail/Sayl
   Sailed/Saild/Saiyled
Salt
Sant Ans/St Ans
sartenly
sarvis
Satorday
savrel/severel
say
   sase
   said
saylors
saymen
sconer   [schooner]
Scothman
Scoundrel
Scuttel
Sean
Seayflour/Seyflour
Seckont/seckond
secured
semed/seamed
send
   sent
Sep   [September]
set   [sat]
Set/set
sey   [sea]
Sey   [see]
   seing
   Sow
   sean
Shares
sharnt   [shan't]
She
   hor, hors
Sheap
shift
Ship
   Ships
   Shiped
shold
shore
short   [shirt]
shot
Shuch   [such]
Shue/shoe
   shoes

shure
shut   [shoot]
Sick
side/syde
Silk
sillonʃed   [silenced]
since
Site   [sight]
sitte   [city]
Sleeap
slitle/slitely/Slytole
Sloope/sloop
  Sloopes
Smol/smorl
Snow
soe/so
sofiʃhont
Sold
sorprysd
Soundance
Southword
  SW
sow   [saw]
speak
  spoke
Spearit
spears
Spit
Spoke
spred
squairʃale
squolle
stade
stand
  Standing
  stud
starbord
starn
staʃined/ʃtaʃhoned
stay
  stade
stear
  steared/Steard
Stil
stones
stop
Storme
stove
story
strained
stream
strength
strike

struck
stud   [stood]
stumps
suffer
Suite/sute
sum/Sum/some
  sum whare/sumwhare
sun   [soon]
Sunday
sundown
sundre
Sun rise
sun set
swelled
swim
swivvol/swivle
  swivvels/swivels
sword
swore
taffel   [taffrail]
tarvern
Taylor, Jeams
teake/take
  taking
  teaken/teakon
  tuck
tel
  tol/told
tendor
thair/thar/thare   [their]
  thare selves
thair/thar/thare/thayr   [there]
thank
that
the
them
then   [than]
then
they/thay
  thair/thar/thare
  them
this/thes
  theas
tho
thote/thot/thorte/thort
thre
thretning
thrs/thurdsday/thursday
thru (thry)
thy [thigh]
thyng/thing
  things
to/two   [to]

tol/told
tomehokes/tome hoaks
top
tops   [topsail]
torte   [taut]
touch
toun
travel
trouʃes/trowʃes
trubbol
trups   [troops]
try
   tryed
the Tryorl   [*Tryon*]
tuck   [took]
turn
turtols
twelve
twice
two   [too]
two   [two]
twors
twoth
twowords   [towards]
tye
   tyed
tyme/time
   tymes
undanted
under
Underwod/Underwood/Unnerwood, Capt
   John
until
up
upon/uppon
us
value
vary/very
ventor   [venture]
veʃsel
villin/villing
voige
vorginne   [Virginia]
waik
wait   [weight]
want
   wornted/wonted
ware/war/wair   [were]
way   [weigh]
way
   wais
Wedonʃday/Wednesday
wee

Owr/our
us
weeak
weged
   weging
   wegges
well
went
Westword
whare/whair
   whairs
wheal
when
whether/whather/wheather
while
White, Artemos/Artenis
who
whot/what
wich/which
Williams, Samuel
wind
windoes
the Wior   [*Weir*]
with
within/with in
with out
wold/would
   woldnot
wolke/wolk
woman
wor   [war]
word
worf
work
wors   [was]
worter
Woʃhingtons, Ginnorl
wotch
   watched
wounded
yankkeas
you
   your
   yourself/your self
yous   [use]
   yoʃeind   [using]
   youʃed